HOMES FOR PEOPLE

100 Years of Council Housing in Birmingham

CARL CHINN

Birmingham Books

First published 1991 by Birmingham Books

Copyright © 1991 Carl Chinn

British Library Cataloguing-in-Publication Data
CPI Catalogue Record for this book is available from the British Library.

ISBN: 0 7093 0172 3

Printed and bound in Great Britain by
BPCC Wheatons Ltd, Exeter

BIRMINGHAM BOOKS

I0621956

Official publishers to Birmingham City Council Library Services
An imprint of Wheaton Publishers Ltd,
a member of the Maxwell Communication Corporation plc

Wheaton Publishers Ltd
Hennock Road, Exeter, Devon EX2 8RP
Tel: 0392 411131

SALES

Direct sales enquiries to Birmingham Books at the address above

I hope that the involvement of so many ordinary Brummies in writing this book proves that history is open to everyone, that it does not belong to professionals alone, and that real history is people's history. In this belief, I dedicate this book to my Nan, Lily Perry, and my aunt, Winnie Martin who, like many Brummies, moved from back-to-backs to council flats. I hope that I have done credit to them and to all those other Brummies who have spent their lives working to provide a better future for their children and grandchildren.

6152

Contents

As with much else in this great city, early industrial growth was to set a seal on the future. In 1821 Birmingham had a population of 106,000; by 1891 it had increased to 429,000. It was therefore, the resulting growth in cheaply built 'back- to-back' houses which would come to shape Birmingham's future housing needs and provision. By the start of the Great War, Birmingham had 43,366 back-to-backs concentrated in the City's central wards. The problems of bad housing and attendant bad health continued into the early 1930s with some 200,000 people living in back-to-backs - a population, at that time, equivalent to Cardiff or Bolton. Indeed it was only with the building of the 1960s estates in Bromford and Castle Vale that the final phase in slum clearance could be achieved.

Although Birmingham's first council houses were built in Ryder Street, Aston, in 1890, the era of large-scale municipal building did not begin until after the end of the Great War. The passing of the 1919 Housing and Town Planning Act, together with Lloyd George's command to build 'homes fit for heroes', soon saw Councils acting to meet their new obligations and the concept of the Council Estate was launched. The first homes were built within the limits of 'old' Birmingham, but with the Government now willing to loan money to Councils, planners soon looked to the city boundary. These 'greenfield' sites on the edge of Birmingham soon gave rise to intensive civic cultivation, and by 1922, over 1,700 homes had been completed despite shortages of materials and labour.

An attitude of municipal pride in the pristine estates was carefully nurtured by the newly created Housing and Estates Department, and a monthly magazine was produced to encourage identification with the estate ethos and to explain the ins and outs of tricky new gadgets such as gas cookers. Tenants' lives were quite extensively ruled by the long list of tenancy regulations which came with a council house and the rent collectors on their weekly rounds also had the role of upholders of the standards set by the Housing Department. This could entail checking of the cleanliness of the home (including that of the bed linen) and seeing that the garden was kept in good order with hedges trimmed to the correct height.

By 1926, Birmingham had built more than 13,000 council houses - more than any other local authority - and this figure had jumped to 40,000 by the time Neville Chamberlain revisited his home town in 1933. However, the Depression began to bite and it took until 1939 for the 50,000th home to be finished.

The start of the Second World War effectively brought to a halt the building programme and drastically worsened the still serious housing shortage. The problem of war damage, added to the numbers of people living in sub-standard housing, led eventually to the passing of the 1944 Town and Country Planning Act. Known as the 'Blitz and Blight Act', it enabled Councils to easily purchase war-damaged and slum properties of which there were many thousands in the inner city areas. In 1947, the City Council used its new powers to purchase the five Central Redevelopment Areas - Ladywood, Lee Bank, Highgate, Newtown and Nechells - and clearance work started immediately. Over 30,000 families were affected by the clearance programme. In addition, a policy of patching - up old properties had to be adopted. In this way previously unfit homes could be given a limited lease of life and many were transformed to provide temporary accommodation for a few more years.

As clearance of the five Central Redevelopment Area sites continued, the debate began about the type of housing the Council should build. In 1951, a City Architect was appointed and the decision was taken to adopt higher densities of homes per acre and to use high-rise blocks as a means to achieve this. There were now over 65,000 people on the waiting list for a council home and, with land in short supply, high rise building was seen as the best way of reconciling need with the space available. Queens Tower in Nechells was one of the first to be built, but the evolving technology of high-rise construction together with the need to build as quickly as possible, meant that the building methods and the resulting shape of blocks changed. The medium-rise and high-rise blocks on an estate like Ladywood were built using new methods of construction called 'system building' - a technique which involved assembling the blocks from panels made at a factory away from the site. This allowed blocks to be built very quickly. These experimental ways of building also extended to some houses of the time.

Although the City Council was not keen to build homes outside the city, the slow start to rebuilding after the war meant that an estate was built over the boundary at Kingshurst in the early 1950s. Despite this and the fast building methods, the waiting list continued to grow and by 1965, 78,000 people were registered. This was largely because the new homes were mainly going to families uprooted by slum clearance and the waiting list continued to grow with the expanding population. The search continued for land for the siting of yet more estates, and a former Second World War airfield on the east of Birmingham was identified for the development of what became (at that time) the City's highest density estate. Castle Vale, built in the mid 1960s, bears witness to a stark declaration of the poplicies of the time, with 34 tower blocks containing nearly a third of the estate's 5000 homes. Although houses continued to be built by the City, such as the award-winning ones at Metchley Grange in Harborne, the dominance of the house as the typical council home had been broken.

Political parties in the 1960s vied with each other over the size of subsidy they were prepared to make available to local authority housing programmes, so the estate building climate continued over into the 1970s. With land becoming ever scarcer, the City Council was forced to build another estate over its boundary at Chelmsley Wood, and then to start building the Frankley estate in Hereford and Worcester. By this time, however, some of the shortcomings of high-rise living were becoming known. Although it was to be a high density estate, Frankley achieved this without resort to high-rise building. Its scale, materials and layout helped to give it a much more human feel than the dwarfing and depersonalising effect typical of some of the estates of only 5-10 years before. It turned out to be the last big estate built by the City, and council building schemes since then have been on a much more modest scale. The land for building vast estates is no longer available and political parties no longer agree on the merit of local authority housing as the best way to meet the country's housing need. In recent years, a steady reduction in the amount of government borrowing approvals to local authorities has meant that resources have had to be channelled away from the building of new homes. This change has coincided with the need to repair and modernise some of the homes on the first council estates and to find solutions to the unexpected problems brought about by non-traditonal construction methods.

As society changes and the balance between age groups in the population alters, new needs arise which must be met. The recent rise in the numbers of older people is a case in point. In 1979, the Housing Department launched a pilot scheme to convert a block of multi-story flats into specially adapted accommodation for older people and so the Vertical Warden Scheme programme began. Other forms of sheltered housing have also been developed and later estates such as Frankley were built with a certain amount of sheltered housing in addition to the usual community facilities. The sheltered housing scheme at Belgrave Middleway, designed by the City Architect's Department, is what is known as 'category 2' sheltered housing and in 1988 it won a top architectural award for the quality of its design. All sheltered accommodation, regardless of type, shares the features of the warden service, an alarm system for emergency use and a common room for social events. When the warden is off duty, a central monitoring service takes alarm calls and ensures that someone goes to help anyone in distress.

In recent years, the Housing Department has led the way in developing new approaches to getting the most out of high-rise housing. Converting tower blocks to sheltered housing and maturity blocks has proved that high-rise living can be problem free. More recently the introduction of the Concierge programme has also improved the quality of life for more of the residents in the City's tower blocks. Each of the five tower blocks in the Highgate scheme, the first integrated concierge development, is linked via infra-red transmission to a control centre. As a result, the on-duty concierge can communicate directly with each entrance, foyer and lift. Much of the technology has been designed and developed in conjunction with the Housing Department, enabling seven concierges to work shifts to maintain security and offer help and advice to tenants twenty-four hours per day, seven days per week, throughout the year.

The publication of Homes for the People marks the centenary of council housing in Birmingham and illustrates the often innovative response to the City's housing problems. Indeed, the story of council housing seems almost to have turned full circle. It has gone from the nineteenth century, when Councils had neither the power nor the inclination to build, through to the massive rise in standards the first council housing achieved and to the 'brave new world' which it was thought only councils could rise to after the war. Another turn of the wheel is seeing the end of council building on any scale.

Councils are no longer the benign dictators they once were, setting standards and intervening in all aspects of tenants' lives. Consultation and choice are now the approaches which characterise the municipal landlord. Tenant relationships and participation in decision-making and management are encouraged through tenants' associations, co-operatives and the network of neighbourhood forums. This spirit of partnership is also evinced in the production of this book, involving as it does many personal contributions from Birmingham people, as well as the successful collaboration of the Housing Department, Library Department and Dr Carl Chinn. I welcome its publication.

Derek Waddington O.B.E.
Director of Housing
Birmingham, 1990

ACKNOWLEDGEMENTS

All writers owe a debt to numerous people who help, encourage and humour them. I am no exception and I should like to acknowledge the assistance of those who have contributed to the publication of this book. Every writer needs a good and committed editorial team, and I was fortunate to have one in Dawn Wise and Steve O'Neill. They have been involved in this project from the start and their support and hard work have been invaluable in putting this book together. I thank them both. Secondly, I acknowledge the essential contributions of Gareth Lewis, who never complained at reproducing so many photographs in such a tight schedule; Lesley Finch, for her tireless research support; Hazel Latta and Marcia Williams for their administrative help; the staff at the Local Studies Department, Birmingham Central Library, who, as usual, assisted in their cheerful and knowledgeable way; and Audrey Horsley who typed my drafts and whose comments on the text I appreciated! I should like to thank, too, Patrick Baird, Maureen McDermott - whose knowledge of housing in Birmingham is encyclopaedic, Des Workman and Tom Houghton for their encouragement and advice; and my wife, Kay, my Mom and Dad and 'Our Kid', Darryl, for their constant support.

When I started to write this book I felt it important that I should include the words of Brummies talking about their homes and their lives. Tony Butler on Radio W.M., the Birmingham Evening Mail and the Daily News helped me appeal for help to do this and I thank them for their interest. Most importantly, I wish to pay tribute to the Brummies who replied to my appeal by sending me photographs, poems and letters about their homes and their lives. They have allowed me to include a working-class voice in this book and I hope that my writing does justice to their vital contribution. My sincere thanks, then, go to: Mrs Adderley; Brenda Batts; Roy Blakey; Susan J. Bodley; Joyce Boxley; Beryl Brookes; Mrs M. Bull; Mrs Busby; Mrs S. P. Cartmell; Nora Clarke; Mrs Clift; Mr Coley; Doreen Cooper; Norman Fearn; Irene Foster; Syd Garrett; Mrs Maisy Harrison; Mr G. R. Hatton; Mrs Hemming; Henry Hughes; Hilda Hughes; Mrs N. E. Jones; Albert Judd; Stan Jukes; Bevan Laing; Mrs McLauchlan; Mrs Malyn; Marjorie Mansell; Winnie Martin; Brian Matthews; Mrs Muckler; P. J. Murray; Lily Need; Mrs Pat Newman; Ada Nicholson; Lily Perry; Edna Piper; Ted Reynolds; Joseph Riley; Edna Scott; Mrs B. L. Smith; Harry Smith; Margaret Smith; M. Stamps; Mr G. W. Stevens; Jim Storey; A. G. Tinley; Mr M. Wareing; Roy White; Arthur Wilkes; and Mrs J. E. Woodfield.

I should like to thank, too, photographers who have allowed me access to their private collections. They are Sylvia Leigh, who kindly made available her marvellous archive of photographs of back-to-backs in the inter-war years; Terry Weir; and Mr L.W Perkins. Finally, I wish to express my gratitude to the following bodies for their thoughtfulness and co-operation in lending photographs which belong to them: the Local Studies Department of Birmingham Central Library, Birmingham City Council Housing Department and The Bournville Village Trust - all of whose contributions have been invaluable; The Birmingham Post and Mail Ltd; Copec; Birmingham Museums and Art Gallery; City of Birmingham Recreations and Community Services; the Archives Department of Birmingham Central Library; Billesley School; and the Hulton-Deutsch Collection. The source of each photograph is indicated in brackets after the caption on the relevant page.

Cover photograph: Children in a courtyard in Summer Lane, Birmingham, in the early 1920s. (Birmingham Library Services)

Chapter 1: The Housing Problem

Many of the old courts are unpaved, and in addition to the puddles of rain water and other worse moisture that stagnate in the holes of the soft and broken surface, they are encumbered with ashes, decaying vegetables and nameless filth.

(Morning Chronicle, newspaper, 1851)

Dilapidated 3-storey back-to-backs in Thomas Street, about 1882; cleared for the development of Corporation Street. (Birmingham Library Services)

In 1821, Birmingham had a population of 106,000; by 1871 it had increased to 343,000 as country people searching for work poured in. They came to a city with no building or planning regulations and which was growing up haphazardly. Like others of the poor, they crowded in to the central areas, where jerry builders had erected cheaply-built structures, mostly of the back-to-back type. Found 'up an entry' and in a courtyard, these houses were tiny, and were separated from their neighbours by a single brick wall. Large families had to make do with two small bedrooms, a living room, and sometimes a cellar. Regularly, dirt and not sand was used in their construction, and the houses were infested with bugs and cockroaches, despite the cleanliness of many families. A pump in the yard, serving up to 400 people, drew smelly and filthy water from underground wells. There was also a brew 'us (wash house), an ashpit for rubbish, and midden privies. These undrained open pieces of ground were used as communal toilets, sometimes by fifteen families, and they were cleaned infrequently. In rainy weather, human refuse overflowed in to the unpaved yards, seeping into the ground and then into the wells. Pig sties and heaps of manure added to this problem and to the stench. Insanitary and unhealthy, Birmingham's courtyards bred disease and quickened death.

1

First elected in 1838, Birmingham's town council became responsible from 1851 for the city's sewerage, drainage and the regulation of sanitary conditions. Two years previously, a concerned observer had warned that urban blight was spreading as stinking courts, ramshackle houses and filthy streets filled in every available plot of land. Unhappily, until 1870, the council was notorious for its inactivity and it spent as little money as possible on its duties. Next to nothing was done to improve the living conditions of the city's poor. Indeed, their problems became worse as the improvements of private developers led to the emergence of Birmingham's central shopping and business area. The city's first great slum clearance came when disreputable streets such as Peck Lane, The Froggery and Old Meeting Street disappeared with the building of first New Street and then Snow Hill Stations (1845-54). It was followed in the 1860s and 1870s by the demolition of squalid property on the Colmore Estate and new rows of imposing buildings emerged around Colmore Row, Edmund Street and Newhall Street. This destruction by the developers improved the appearance of the city and rid it of unhealthy slums, but their motive was profit not concern for the plight of the poor. Neither they nor the council gave any thought to rehousing those made homeless by their schemes. The poor had to crowd ever more tightly in to the swathe of slums which were emerging as a collar around the city centre.

Public improvements which should ameliorate the condition of the poor, are often one of their great afflictions. Their dwellings are razed to make way for more remunerative structures.

(James Hole, The Homes of the Working Classes, 1866)

Small houses and workshops in Edmund Street, about 1870; demolished for the building of the Art Gallery and the School of Art. Notice the Town Hall in the background, built 1833-35. (Birmingham Library Services)

Towards the end of the 'sixties a few Birmingham men made the discovery that perhaps a strong and able Town Council might do almost as much to improve the conditions of life in the town as Parliament itself. . . They spoke of sweeping away streets in which it was not possible to live a healthy and decent life; of making the town cleaner, sweeter and brighter.   (Robert Dale, in R.A. Armstrong, Henry William Crosskey, 1895)

Slum dwellings and sodden yard in John Street, 1875; cleared for the development of Corporation Street. (The Graphic, 1876 - an illustrated newspaper)

Problems of bad housing, inadequate sanitation, and ill health were not unique to Birmingham. The poor everywhere lived in life-destroying districts. However, once started an epidemic did not respect wealth; cholera, diphtheria, scarlet fever, typhus, and other diseases killed the rich as well. Fear, and a Christian conscience pricked by the dreadful living conditions suffered by the poor, led Parliament to pass laws aimed at improving health. Unfortunately, most were not compulsory, local authorities adopted them only if they wished. Some did so vigorously. In 1847, Liverpool appointed the country's first medical officer of health, and then made serious attempts to improve its supplies of gas and water. Birmingham was more sluggish in its response to the problems posed by unplanned urban growth, but by the late 1860s a belief in a Civic Gospel had taken hold of many affluent men and they urged councillors to become more energetic. Inspired by preachers like Dawson and Dale, they realised that the council needed some control over the development of Birmingham, and they believed that they had a duty to make life better for its poor. Their policy demanded that money be spent, and by the early 1870s they had overcome opposition and were in a position of strength on the council.

In the 1800s most governments believed in individualism and 'letting things be'. Birmingham's reformers knew that such inaction would not help the poor, that some interference in citizens' lives was necessary for the welfare of the community. They argued that public services vital for good health ought to be owned by the local authority and controlled by the elected representatives of the people. Under Joseph Chamberlain as mayor (1873-1876) this belief in municipal socialism led the council to take control of the city's gas and water companies. At the same time landlords were forced to close polluted wells and to connect their properties with the town water supply, usually via a standpipe in each yard; the sewage farm at Saltley was improved and extended; a drainage board was established; and unhealthy open middens began to be replaced by toilets with a metal pan under each seat. These were emptied weekly by the council, as were the 'miskins' - wooden tubs put in each yard for the collection of dry ashes and rubbish. From 1872, the city's health was monitored by Dr Hill, its first medical officer, who reported to a Health Committee from 1875, and sanitary inspectors were appointed to deal with 'nuisances', ranging from adulterated food and infectious diseases to filthy courts. The horrendous problems of slum life could be ignored no longer.

All who know anything of Birmingham . . . know how very much remains to be done before Birmingham can be considered either a healthy or a clean town, and before the lower portions of it inhabited by the working classes . . . can be regarded as fit for their occupation. (William White, Report of the Improvement Committee, 1875).

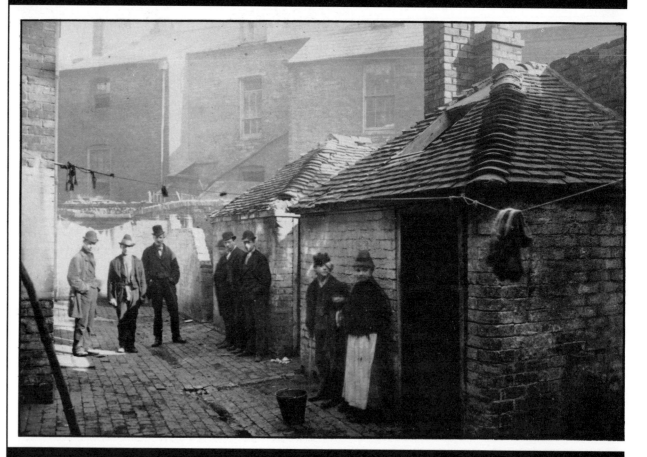

No. 1 Court, Thomas Street, about 1882; cleared for the development of Corporation Street. Notice the 'billycocks' - bowler hats - worn by the men.
(Birmingham Library Services)

The Gullett, 1875; a notorious narrow lane cleared for the development of Corporation Street.
(The Graphic, 1876 - an illustrated newspaper)

Ill health and bad housing were the twin evils which bedevilled and blighted the lives of the city's poor. The link between the two was inextricable. Each year in the poverty stricken St. Mary's Ward, twice as many people died as did in the prosperous Edgbaston Ward. The evidence was conclusive. Poverty killed. Aware that bad housing harmed health, the council passed a by-law in 1876 which effectively forbade the building of back-to-backs, but the dreadful conditions in one of the city's vilest slums prompted more drastic measures. This was a collection of gullets (narrow lanes) in St. Mary's Ward, where 10-12,000 people survived in housing that was in a state of dangerous dilapidation and which was unfit for human habitation. Under an act of 1875, corporations had been given the power to acquire, demolish and redevelop slum areas, and the council used this law to make the area the subject of an improvement scheme. Property was compulsory purchased and cleared, and a wide road - Corporation Street - was formed. By 1889 it was filled with fine new buildings, reflecting Birmingham's dignity and position as the metropolis of the Midlands. Yet, as the prestigious new street advanced, the plight of those who had lived there was ignored. A slum was erased, but once again no provision was made to re-house those whom progress had made homeless.

The council had appointed an Improvement Committee to oversee the removal of slum buildings and the construction in their place of the Parisian-style boulevard in Corporation Street. Permission could have been sought from the government to build working-class housing on some of the cleared sites. It was not. Condemnation grew at the lack of concern shown by the council for the poor who had been ejected from their homes without any choice or any say. In 1885 the committee was prompted to action by the charge that only middle-class residents had benefited from the improvement. A plan was prepared for the erection of flats for working-class people in Dalton Street. Despite some vigorous support, the council rejected it, believing that private developers would build houses to replace those removed. By 1889 the disinterest of the private sector was glaring, so the committee proposed building twenty-two houses in Ryder Street, on a site left vacant for development since 1883. The scheme was small-scale - 855 dwellings had been demolished by the improvement scheme - and it did nothing to solve the housing problems of the poor, yet it encountered considerable opposition before it was passed. Built at a cost of £182 each, the houses were finished in September 1890 and were rented out at 5s 6d a week.

Mrs Annie Storey and daughter, Maisie, back of 63, Ryder Street, 1949/50; Birmingham's 1st council houses, built 1890. (Mrs Maisie Harrison and Mr Jim Storey)

It is little to the credit of the men who have managed the municipal affairs of Birmingham that not one artisan's dwelling has been built out of the £1,800,000 which has been spent on the new street, and therefore that wretched and unwholesome dwellings, which still remain standing, are overcrowded to a fearful extent.

(St. James' Gazette, newspaper, 1885)

Lawrence Street council houses, late 1960s; built 1891, demolished 1971. (Bournville Village Trust)

The Ryder Street houses were let quickly, encouraging the committee in 1891 to make a more extensive proposal for nearby Lawrence Street. Costing £172 each, eighty-two similar houses were built, rented at between 5s and 7s 6d a week. Despite the objections of those opposed to public involvement in housing, the council had shown that it was able to compete successfully with private enterprise. It had built good quality houses, let at moderate rents, and without serious loss to the ratepayers. Still, neither scheme addressed the problem of slum housing. They were limited actions responding to criticism, doing nothing to improve the living conditions of the poor. Firstly, the houses were let to families of a 'good class' - only 'respectable', well-paid working-class people were wanted as tenants, not the poor. Secondly, even the lowest rental of 5s a week was too much for a poor family. In 1884 it was reported that there were 27,000 houses in Birmingham let at 3s 6d a week or less, and the great majority were insanitary and defective. They ought to have been demolished, and the council had the powers to do so. However, wide-scale slum clearance had to be accompanied by a massive programme of building houses cheap enough to rent by the poor. If not, terrible overcrowding would result. Such a plan meant huge subsidies from the council, and no profit. The council was not yet prepared to accept this.

In 1893, Dr Alfred Hill, Birmingham's Medical Officer of Health, inspected the sanitary condition of two poor areas, Woodcock Street and Milk Street. His report could have applied to most neighbourhoods in the central parts of the city. None of the property was good. The houses were back-to-back, with dilapidated roofs, floors, sinks, walls and wash-houses. They were damp, having leaky roofs and porous quarries as floors, and they were without damp-courses; whilst the yards were unpaved and sodden with filth. The buildings of the districts were badly arranged, so that they were crowded closely together, and some were obstructive; for example, the first house in number one court Milk Street was only seven feet from other dwellings. Dr Hill concluded that the construction of the houses in both localities led to a lack of light and fresh air. Together with the damp and generally bad drainage and sewerage, this caused a danger to the health of the poor who lived there. Two years later he provided tragic statistical evidence for this conclusion. After taking a population census for the Milk Street area, he estimated that its death rate was twice as high as the average for the city. He recommended that the only remedy for the district was to make it subject to an improvement scheme which would re-arrange and re-construct its streets and houses.

. . . I am therefore of the opinion that the narrowness, closeness, bad arrangement, and bad condition of the houses . . . the want of light, air and ventilation, and other sanitary defects, are dangerous to the health of the inhabitants of the buildings . . . (Dr Hill, Annual Report, Medical Officer of Health, 1893)

Decrepit 3-storey back to backs, no. 15 Court, Milk Street, about 1905.
(Birmingham Library Services)

The Council had accepted as a duty the carrying out of the intentions of the Acts of Parliament to `provide some accommodation for the class of persons displaced in the interest of Public Health', but it did it with no enthusiasm.

(Asa Briggs, History of Birmingham, Vol II, 1952)

Milk Street council flats, mid 1960s; finished in 1900, demolished 1966.
(Bournville Village Trust)

The Housing of the Working Classes Act of 1890 allowed the council to prepare improvement schemes outside the Corporation Street area. Consequently, in 1894 Dr Hill's recommendation was accepted by the Improvement Committee. It was proposed to compulsory purchase the buildings in those parts of the Woodcock Street and Milk Street areas which were declared as insanitary, to demolish them and build 116 houses upon the sites. Because of the cost involved in buying the scheduled buildings, there was determined opposition to this plan within the council. As a compromise, the unhealthy houses in Woodcock Street were dropped from the scheme. In 1895 Parliament approved the proposal for Milk Street, and within two years, half of the site of 65 dwellings and a few workshops was cleared for building, and the remainder was unoccupied. Plans were drawn up to replace them with 64 dual-system houses, each of three rooms, with rents of 4s 3d on the lower tier and 3s 9d on the upper. The committee was satisfied that this was the only way to build homes in the City, at a rental low enough for labourers and without a loss to the rate-payers. A majority of councillors objected vehemently to the plan and it was withdrawn. Finally, in 1898 it was agreed to construct four two-storey blocks of tenements. The 61 homes of between two and four rooms were finished in 1900 and let at between 3s and 5s a week.

As the twentieth century dawned, the lifestyle of the poor worsened. The council was empowered to demolish the most insanitary houses, or else order owners to improve them. Since 1891, it had cleared 536 dwellings, and more were closed by owners unable or unwilling to make the sanitary improvements demanded of them. Without a building programme to replace the houses lost, overcrowding increased and rents for slum dwellings rose. Some councillors realised this, arguing that destruction could not continue without immediate and wide-scale construction, and in 1900 the Health Committee reported that a new and large housing scheme was needed. It bought 17 acres of land at Bordesley Green, planning to build there 621 houses - at rents between 3s 9d and 5s a week. Additionally, two, four-storey blocks of tenements were to be erected on a plot in Potter Street. Sadly, many councillors resisted fiercely a policy of municipal house-building. The Potter Street Scheme passed in to oblivion, and in 1908 the site at Bordesley Green was leased to the Ideal Benefit Society. Good quality houses were built, but they were too costly for the poor to rent. Birmingham's housing problem remained - thousands of insanitary back-to-backs which could not be demolished until decent houses were built at a rent cheap enough for the city's poor.

I am still of the opinion that the accommodation for the labouring classes is altogether inadequate, and that until a large number of dwellings for labourers are built, it would be unwise to close any considerable number of the existing houses, although many of them are not really fit to live in.
(Dr Hill, Annual Report, Medical Officer of Health, 1900).

No. 4., back of 99, Hill Street, with its wooden shutters to the windows and the gas lamp lighting the dark and narrow entry leading to the street; about 1905.
(Birmingham Library Services)

The pen of a Zola could scarcely do justice to the filthy horrors of this slum in Christian England, and in the best-governed city in the world, with the finest Health Committee and the most enterprising municipality ever known.

(J. Cuming-Walters, Scenes in Slumland, 1901)

Two-storey back-to-backs, 4-7 Lincoln Place, Garrison Lane, about 1905. Notice the nets on the ground-floor windows, indicating the valiant efforts made by housewives to improve their dreadfully-built homes. (Birmingham Library Services)

During the 1870s and 1880s, Birmingham had seemed set on transforming the living conditions of its poor. Many landlords were ordered to improve their ramshackle properties, and between them the council and private enterprise had destroyed some of the city's worst slums. Gas supplies were laid on; polluted wells were filled in and fresh water piped to taps centrally-placed in courtyards; midden privies were replaced with pan closets as sewerage and drainage were improved; and by-laws forbade the dumping of refuse on streets. These improvements in sanitation led to a marked fall in the city's death rate from 25.2 deaths for every thousand people between 1871-75 to 20.7 by 1881-85. The dynamism of Joseph Chamberlain seemed to animate the council, and the city appeared progressive and innovative. Once reproached as 'blackest Birmingham', now it was eulogised as 'the best-governed city in the world.' Yet, the task of improvement was only half-done. The council set its face resolutely against a policy of massive slum clearance and of building council houses on a large scale. Inevitably, inaction led to deteriorating conditions in the poorer parts of Birmingham. Apart from a few concerned churchmen and councillors, there seemed little interest in the misery of the poor. Indeed, many better-off people presumed that slums had disappeared from enlightened Birmingham, and were but a distant memory. Soon they were to be shocked out of their complacency.

Back-to-backs were built in Birmingham from the late 1700s. Most had three rooms - although some were two storeys high and others were three - and they came to dominate the city's central areas. By 1914 there were 43,366 of them grouped in about 6,000 courts. During the 1890s Dr Hill, as Birmingham's medical officer, urged their clearance, and in 1899 he explained vividly how they harmed life. Most back-to-backs were rented at 3s 6d or less a week. In St. Bartholomew's Ward over 50% of the houses were in this category, and out of every 1,000 people in the district, 32.7 died each year. In areas where there were no such houses, the death rate was dramatically lower, 17.1 per thousand. Each year because of insanitary, badly-built, back-to-back houses, 3,000 people died who would have lived if given better housing. More horrific than even these distressing figures were those relating to the death rate amongst babies. In St. Bartholomew's Ward in 1904, out of every 1,000 babies born, 331 died before the age of one. By contrast, in Edgbaston the infant mortality rate was 133. The conclusion was inescapable. Poverty murdered. The birth right of the poor was a higher death rate; their inheritance the dreadful conditions in which they struggled to live. Birmingham's council could not continue to ignore their bitter cry.

It is impossible to doubt that houses hidden away in close confined courts out of sight of all except their inmates, beyond the reach of currents of fresh air such as sweep the open streets, beyond the influence also of sunlight . . . are most prejudicial . . . to the physical health. (Dr Hill, Annual Report, Medical Officer of Health, 1899)

Nos. 1 & 2, no. 2 Court, Tower Street, Summer Lane, about 1905. Bottom left, notice the cellar - built for storage but often unusable because of damp and partial flooding. (Birmingham Library Services)

May God awaken those within this parish and those outside it, to a sense of duty, so that such neighbourhoods may no longer be left in their darkness but may be illuminated by 'The Light of Light'. *(Rev. Bass, Everyday in Blackest Birmingham, 1898)*

Nos. 4-6, no. 2 Court, St. James's Place, about 1905. Notice the closeness of the railway line to the houses. (Birmingham Library Services)

In 1898 the Reverend T. J. Bass wrote a book describing the poverty and terrible environment in the parish of St. Laurence, Gosta Green. He failed in his heartfelt attempt to outrage and arouse public opinion, but in 1901 a journalist called J. Cuming Walters succeeded with a series of explicit articles for the Birmingham Daily Gazette. Called Scenes in Slumland, they made a number of shocking revelations. Five aldermen were denounced as owners of slum property and, more perfidiously, so was the Deputy Chairman of the Health Committee. In a blatant breach of trust in his position, he used one of the committee's officials to collect his rents and to intercept reports on the state of his property. A furore was caused by these disclosures, and those relating to the appalling conditions put up with by poor people. Cuming Walters was sued for libel, but the indignation of the citizens of Birmingham was woken and there was sustained agitation demanding that action be taken on the housing question. In June, 1901, this led to a bad-tempered debate in the council. The evidence connecting bad housing to ill health and high mortality seemed overwhelming, yet there remained a large number of councillors convinced that they need not take vigorous action. Fortunately, they were defeated and by 32 votes to 30 the council agreed to set up a new Housing Committee. It appeared that the bitter cry of the poor had been heeded.

The new Housing Committee took over all powers the council exercised under the housing Acts and such powers under the Public Health Acts as thought desirable. Its chairman was the energetic J. S. Nettlefold, but he dashed any hopes of a large-scale programme of building council houses in Birmingham. Like the majority of his committee, he believed that such a scheme would check private enterprise which it was still thought would provide the solution to the housing question. Instead, what was derogatorily called a policy of 'slum patching' was embarked on. Owners of dilapidated property were ordered to remedy sanitary and drainage defects, put damp courses in, open windows, and repair roofs, floors and walls. Alongside this policy was one of limited demolition of slum dwellings for one of two reasons. Firstly, where repairs were not carried out; secondly, to open up a courtyard to light and air by knocking down the house on either side of its entry. Courtyards affected in this manner became known as 'Nettlefold Courts'. Between 1901 and 1906, 1,132 houses were made fit to live in, 522 were demolished, and 41 courts were opened to the street. It was admitted that this policy was not drastic, but it remained unchanged until 1914.

A few houses have been so far renovated as to be not quite unfit for human habitation, and a few courts opened up to admit a modicum of light and air. Mr Nettlefold has spoken of the result as the transformation of the slums into light and airy terraces, but the fact is that the houses themselves remain . . . dark, inconvenient and such as no member of the Council would care to inhabit. . .

(J. A. Fellows and Fred Hughes, The Housing Question in Birmingham, 1905)

Improvement of 2-storey back-to-backs, no. 11 Court, rear of 80, Aston Road; about 1908. Notice the addition of bay windows, the fitting of new doors and roofs and the installation of proper drainage facilities. (Birmingham Library Services)

> I feel I must reiterate the opinion expressed in previous reports, that it is useless to look for any great diminution in the death rate of Birmingham, until, among other measures, more provision has been made for light and ventilation in its crowded wards.
>
> (Dr Robertson, Annual Report, Medical Officer of Health, 1905)

A Nettlefold Court. No. 2 Court, William Street after reconstruction and opening up of the yard to the street; about 1909. (Birmingham Library Services)

In Birmingham's poorer neighbourhoods the housing stock was ageing and deteriorating. Faced with mounting structural and sanitary problems, the policy of slum patching could be no more than a short-term measure. However, until enough councillors recognised the need for slum clearance and council house building it was the only way in which the lives of poor people could be improved. Together with better health care, it led to a fall in both infant mortality and the general death rates in the city's poverty stricken central wards. This improvement should be acknowledged but not exaggerated. The poor remained more likely to die than the better off, just because they were poor and lived in slum housing. This was shown graphically by an investigation in 1909 and 1910 in the depressed wards of St. Stephen's and St. George's. It divided the population according to the weekly income of the head of the household. In that group where the wage was 20s a week or more, the infant mortality rate was 140; in the group where the income was less than 20s a week, this rose distressingly to 210. Further, the babies of the poorer section who survived to the age of twelve months were, on average, 1lb less in weight than the babies born to more prosperous parents. Clearly, life expectancy and health were impaired by a low income and the rent of an insanitary house.

Despite drainage improvements after 1901, sanitation in the courtyards of Birmingham remained appalling. Allegedly 'competent witnesses' felt that a common tap in the courtyard and a neighbouring gulley were sufficient to provide water for all its residents and to drain away the slop water. Dr Robertson, Birmingham's Medical Officer of Health from 1903, disagreed. He argued that each house needed its own sink and water supply as a minimal requirement, if poor people were to win their battle for cleanliness. Still, common taps remained widespread, and a few vile, unhealthy midden privies remained. Irregularly cleaned, human refuse overspilled from them in to courtyards and houses. From the 1870s most were replaced by dry privies with a pan below the seat. Supposedly emptied once a week, they were shared by several families, and were inadequate, smelly, unhealthy, and lacking in privacy. Little wonder with such deficient facilities that disease was rife in poorer neighbourhoods and that diarrhoea slaughtered so many children unnecessarily. Healthier water closets were universal in middle-class houses, but they were not introduced in to courtyards because the city's Water Department had an insufficient supply of water. This class-biased reason disappeared upon completion of the Elan Valley works in 1904, and water closets began to replace dry pan privies in the slums.

At the end of the yard stood three ashcans and five lavatories, or closets as we called them. These each consisted of a square box with a large round hole in the middle. Us children had to hold the sides of the seat otherwise we could have fallen in. These were dry closets. You can imagine the stench in the summer.

(Kathleen Dayus, Camden Street, Hockley, Her People, 1982)

Communal toilets in central Birmingham, about 1920. Notice the water closet in the middle and the 2 dry pan privies on either side; also the memorial on the house wall, commemorating local men who died in The First World War.

(Birmingham Library Services)

Not all had despaired of change, with many making every effort to enable their humble homes to be clean and pleasant in appearance, to do them credit with no modern aids available, just soap and water plus elbow grease.

(Walter Chinn, Studley Street, Sparkbrook, In Victoria's Image, n.d.)

Women maiding the washing with a maid (dolly) in the maiding tub, then mangling it; outside the communal brew 'us (wash-house), no 6 Court, Hanley Street, early 1920s. Another photograph indicating the heroic efforts made by poor women to maintain cleanliness in adverse circumstances. (Bournville Village Trust)

For outsiders, a slum was not just bad housing but a way of life. Slummie became a derogatory term evoking a picture of dirty, rough and unpleasant people. In reality, there was more heroism in poorer neighbourhoods than ever can be assessed. Tens of thousands of people fought to survive with dignity a life of low pay, ill-health, under-nourishment and inadequate housing. Too often, observers from another class were oblivious to their continuous battle against a hostile environment. Those who employed poor women to do their washing and cleaning could never comprehend the hard work involved in staying clean. Dirty clothes had to be maided with a dolly in a tub, and then scrubbed in a smaller one - arduous tasks in themselves. Then the clothes were boiled in the copper in the brew 'us. This held about twenty gallons of water, filled by the bucketful from the tap in the yard - whatever the weather. Next, washing was swilled in a tub of water and Reckitt's Blue, then starched. This was followed by mangling, hanging out and ironing. Finally, water from the copper was used to scrub wooden toilet seats, stairs and floorboards. Other heavy cleaning tasks for wives included black-leading the grate, polishing brasses, whitening the hearth, and red ochreing the front step. Surrounded by factories belching out smoke and dirt, the wonder is that so many women won their never-ending battle against dirt.

Since the 1860s, speculative builders had erected houses in outlying districts for the better-paid of the working class. By the 1880s, areas like Sparkbrook were mostly covered with six-roomed tunnel-back dwellings, each with its own back garden and toilet - although no bathroom. Migration was encouraged by the building of suburban factories and by bicycles, trams and railways which enabled workers to live further than walking distance from their jobs. Increasingly, the central wards of Birmingham were left to the poor. Before 1914 the poverty line was acknowledged to be an income of 18s-21s a week. Unskilled workers in regular jobs were unlikely to earn this, and for most labourers employment was irregular. Daily they searched for the casual work more likely to be found in the workshops and factories crowding the central areas than in the suburbs. They had no choice; they had to live near the available jobs, in houses cheap enough for them to rent. The unskilled were caught in an unenviable position. Too poor to move, the council's housing policy led to fewer houses and increased rents. In 1905 the Health Department recorded a sample of 243 houses it had dealt with. Demolitions had reduced the number to 226, whilst average rents had risen from 3s 8d a week to 4s 3d. Consequently, tenants were paying interest on half the cost of the landlord's repairs on their properties. The straitjacket of poverty was pulled tighter.

Why don't I leave? Because I can't get a house any better near to my husband's work, or near the school the children go to. We've got no choice. We're obliged to take the houses we can afford . .
(Birmingham woman, Scenes in Slumland, 1901)

Garden in court in Sherbourne Road, Balsall Heath, near to Longmore Street, Mrs Gilbert sits beside her daughter Ethel, also pictured are another daughter Elizabeth and son Edwin (Ted), about 1910. Despite the unfavourable conditions, many poor people cultivated lovely gardens. (Mr A. G. Tinley, son of Ethel)

No. 7 Court, Cheapside, about 1905, showing communal water pump with a jug beside it; washing lines leading from the brew 'us; the cobblestones of the yard; and young children using axes to chop up firewood. Afterwards, it would be bundled and sold to raise money for the family. (Birmingham Library Services)

In 1904, a report on the 10,000 people of the Floodgate Street area revealed a death rate 60% higher than the city's average; and in Park Street it was a grim 63 per 1,000 people compared to 12.1 in Edgbaston. Not surprisingly, two thirds of houses in the street were back-to-backs and most of the men were unskilled labourers and street traders earning between 17s and 21s a week. The conclusion was unequivocal. Wages in the central wards made it impossible for a labourer to keep a wife and family out of poverty. To earn enough just for rent, clothing and fuel, wives and children had to work. The jobs open to them were ill-paid, tiring and repetitive: wrapping up hair pins in paper - 10 to the paper with 1 outside to hold the pack together - at 2d a 1,000; carding safety pins at 2d a gross if there were 9 pins of different sizes on each card; and varnishing pen-holders at 1d a gross. Other laborious tasks involved selling firewood, carding of hooks and eyes, and the sewing of buttons on to cards - the wages for which could only be calculated in 'infinitesimal fractions of pence.' Mothers and children had to take sweated jobs to stave off starvation and stay out of the hated workhouse. They had to live in decrepit back-to-backs close to their work, which was found in the central wards not the healthier suburbs.

Escape from the meshes of poverty was rare. Poor people could only afford harmful housing, and that had to be near the firms which provided casual and sweated employment. In the central wards, back-to-backs vied for space with works, warehouses, shops, railway lines and canal wharfs. Factories and workshops were common in courtyards, and often houses were not even separated structurally from them. This proximity damaged further the health of poor people. Industry made the atmosphere smoky, dirty, gloomy and sunless, it discharged poison, and it masked overcrowding in the deprived wards. In 1908 the number of persons per acre in St. Stephen's Ward was 132.7, and in St. George's it was 162.1. This compared to an average for the city of 44.2. However, works of various kinds were numerous in both districts, so that these density figures did not represent the true crowding of space. The real nature of the problem of overcrowding was highlighted by the atrocious situation in the Oxygen Street area. This district, which included Great Lister, Adams, Heanage and Dartmouth Streets, comprised 14 acres, of which only 8 was occupied by housing. Here, 2,429 people crowded in to 589 dwellings, giving a population density of 272 persons per acre of inhabited land, 6 times as much as the average for the city. Together with bad housing, the nearness of industry, and poverty, this abominable overcrowding in the area led to twice as many deaths each year as in Birmingham as a whole.

In Oxygen Street - ye gods, what a name for a street where atmosphere, polluted by neighbouring works, made my throat and nose smart and eyes run - the houses were amongst the worst I have ever seen. (Rev. Bass, Down East Amongst the Poorest, 1904)

102-104 Bagot Street, about 1905, indicating the closeness of factories to homes - Canning remains a Birmingham firm. Notice the tiny entry to Court no. 6 and the two barefooted children on the left. (Birmingham Library Services)

We only had two bedrooms. Four in a bed, top and bottom. Lads in the same room. 'Cus there was only Billy and Georgie lads, but as they got older they had to sleep downstairs.

(Lily Perry, Whitehouse Street, Aston)

No. 15 Court, Adams Street, about 1905. This was one of Birmingham's poorest streets, but notice the spotlessly clean woman and child in the background.
(Birmingham Library Services)

The survey of the Oxygen Street area had indicated that each household numbered 4.1 people. This statistic from a desperately poor neighbourhood seemed to confirm the belief that in Birmingham the overcrowding of houses was not a problem. Such statistics were misleading, simply because they represented an average. The high birth rate in poorer districts ensured that many households greatly exceeded four in number. Large families were common, and children had to sleep top and tail in the cramped two-bedroomed accommodation of back-to-backs, with fathers and older brothers often sleeping in the single room downstairs. In some homes poverty led to the taking in of lodgers to help pay the rent, and overcrowding was made worse. The problem was exacerbated by a shortage of housing in the central areas, which became obvious by 1913. Demolition of insanitary property increased after the passing of the Housing and Town Planning Act, 1909, and by 1911, in St.Bartholomew's Ward alone, there were 874 houses fewer than in 1896. Similar great decreases were recorded for the other central wards of St. Mary's, Market Hall, St. Paul's, St. Thomas's, St.Martin's St. Stephen's and St. George's. Economic reasons ensured that most of the poor made homeless could not move to the suburbs. Consequently, the demand rose on the remaining houses in the centre. Rents went up and overcrowding increased. Unless the demolished houses were replaced quickly by cheap and decent housing, the problem could only deteriorate.

Although Birmingham's housing policy was fixed firmly, councillors were interested in other approaches to solving the housing question. In 1905 a Deputation from the Housing Committee visited Berlin and six other German cities. In the same year, an enquiry including W. J. Davis, the renowned Brummie trade-union leader, compared the lives of the city's brassworkers with those of the German capital. Both groups thought that German children were better dressed, tended and mannered, and that the lifestyle of the workers was more 'wholesome' than that of the Brummie working class. Nettlefold's group felt that the German houses they visited were cleaner and tidier, but it disliked the preponderance of flats, and found the accommodation inferior to that of Birmingham. It believed that the lighting, ventilation, and sanitary conditions of the houses were worse, and that the average room space occupied by each family was smaller. It might be wondered at how bad the German flats were if back-to-backs were considered superior to them. Yet, one important lesson was learned from the Germans - the significance of town planning. The Deputation recommended that the council should seek larger powers to control the building of new areas, aiming to ensure a better distribution of houses and the building of wide arterial roads for through traffic. Also, it advised the council to buy and lay out land in the suburbs, mark out open spaces, and encourage the building of houses at a rental available for working-class people. The proposals were approved. They signified the beginning of the Town Planning Movement in England.

22

Town planning on lines similar to those so successful in Germany would materially assist the creation of open spaces. (Housing Committee Report, 1906)

Cutting rods in the bedstead trade at Fisher Brown & Co. Ltd, Lionel Street, 1902.
(Birmingham Library Services)

The first houses on the Bournville Estate, at 232-222, Maryvale Road - with building going on in the background; 1895. Contrast these fine houses with the ramshackle back-to-backs in which poor Brummies lived. (Bournville Village Trust)

Town planning of the kind envisaged by the Housing Committee was present in the Birmingham region, but it was not directed by the council. The Cadbury brothers decided to move their chocolate works from the city to the open fields of Bournville in 1879, believing that it would be better for their work people to live in the country. In 1895, to make houses available to them, George Cadbury bought 140 acres of land near the factory and developed it. Unlike the jerry-built, unhealthy back-to-backs of Birmingham which were erected without any thought of town planning, these houses were well-built, spacious, sanitary and open to the light and air. They were grouped in pairs, threes, or fours and set back 20 feet from wide, tree-lined roads. There were gardens to the front, vegetable gardens at the back, and one-tenth of the estate was reserved for open spaces. Initially, 143 houses were sold on ground leases of 999 years - to prevent infilling on the gardens; and later more were built to rent. This careful town planning had astounding effects: in 1915, Bournville's infant mortality rate was 47, compared to 187 in St. Mary's Ward, whilst the general death rate was 8 compared to 24.5. But the poor did not share in the benefits of Bournville. It was not intended for them, rather the better-paid of the working class, those thought respectable and worthy. For the poor, fresh air, a healthy environment, and decent housing remained unattainable.

Encouraged by the German example and by Bournville, the idea of municipal town planning took hold in Birmingham. Indeed, the term itself was coined in the city in 1906 at talks in the office of Dr Robertson. With the zeal of converts, he and Councillor Nettlefold then began discussions with housing reformers in other towns, sending out 'missionaries' to explain the benefits of their concept. Following a conference in Manchester, the idea was taken up nationally and in 1909 a Housing and Town Planning Act was passed. This empowered municipalities to make town-planning schemes regarding land that was under development, subject to the approval of a national board. The vision of the pioneers of the town planning movement was to transform the dismal industrial towns of England in to pleasant garden cities, built according to the Bournville model. Yet, to realise this dream fully, councils would have to build municipal houses and spend vast sums of money. Birmingham was not ready to do this. Most councillors now recognised that the city had to supervise - and to an extent control - the character of new development, if only to prevent the emergence of new slums. They remained to be persuaded that the most vital aspect of town planning was the building of corporation houses.

Let us then, picture the Birmingham of the future as a city with fine radial tree-planted roads, with public squares, open gardens and recreation grounds, with its circular boulevard, and its setting of park lands and garden suburbs, from which the jerry builder and the smoke have been banished, and where the air is pure and fresh . . .

(W. H. Bidlake, Birmingham As It Might Be, 1911)

Moor Pool Avenue, Harborne Tenants Ltd, 1966. Though less well-known than Bournville, the 500 houses of this estate - developed from 1909 - are another example of planned housing development in Birmingham. (Birmingham Library Services)

House back of 22, Blews Street, about 1905, showing a warning notice about diarrhoea - a terrible killer of poor children before 1914.
(Birmingham Library Services)

Debate about the direction town planning should take in Birmingham was sterile. Quite simply, the city lacked the space for any effective town planning policy. It had few parks or playgrounds - in the Floodgate Street area only the unsuitable Park Street Gardens catered for 2,600 local children. Certainly, there were no vacant plots left for large-scale house-building or for the development of garden villages. Dr Robertson in particular recognised that the population pressure on the over-crowded central wards had to be relieved. He argued that this could be done only if decent, low-rent houses were built on undeveloped sites outside the city boundary, although he did not specify by whom. Furthermore, he understood that poorer people would not move to a new estate unless they could return to the city for work via a rapid and cheap transport system. His far-sighted scheme gained increasing support, but it could not be achieved unless Birmingham extended its boundaries and gained the acres of undeveloped land available in adjoining boroughs. In 1911 this occurred and the city swallowed up Aston, Erdington, Handsworth, Kings Norton and Northfield and Yardley. The importance of this extension cannot be exaggerated. Birmingham's size increased by 30,000 acres, 24,000 of which was not fully developed. This land would allow the council to tackle the housing question with vigour once it had accepted the need for municipal housing. A town planning scheme was the first step in that direction.

At its own request, the small parish of Quinton was incorporated in to Birmingham in 1909. The following year the council initiated the city's first town planning scheme under the 1909 Act, and in 1913 it became the first in the country to be accepted by the government. It covered Quinton, Harborne and Edgbaston, and it provided the model for later schemes in areas annexed by the city in 1911, and for other local authorities. The 838 acres of Quinton were mostly undeveloped, and the scheme prohibited manufactories, scheduling it only for residential building. There were three reasons for this: firstly, the absence of railway lines; secondly, because the district lay to the west and prevailing winds would have carried factory smoke over Edgbaston and other residential districts; and thirdly, because it was a desirable place to live. Not more than 12 houses were to be built per acre, compared to 18 per acre in recently-developed Sparkhill and where there had not been a town planning scheme; and two areas each in Harborne and Quinton were set apart for parks and open spaces. However, whilst the council made 9 of the area's 23 streets, it built none of the houses. The Quinton scheme was followed quickly by the East Birmingham Scheme, also approved in 1913, covering 1,443 acres in Saltley, Washwood Heath, Little Bromwich and Small Heath. The district was laid out for factories and houses - the latter at a density of between 12 to 18 an acre - and 51 acres was set aside for allotments. Once more, there was no municipal building.

The area newly added to the City by the annexation of the parish of Quinton offered a very favourable field for the first experiment.

(C. A. Vince, History of the Corporation of Birmingham, Vol IV, 1923)

Farmland at Quinton, 1920s-1930s. (Birmingham Library Services)

Back of Colmore Flats, Hospital Street, Summer Lane; one of only two blocks of flats erected in Birmingham by private builders before 1914. (Bournville Village Trust)

Birmingham's housing question demanded a radical solution. Those acute to the poor's problems knew the remedy lay with the council. Municipal houses had to be built - small, plain, inexpensive and within easy reach of the city centre. Instead, the Council's policy of slum patching and demolition expected private enterprise to supply the answer to rebuilding. It did not, bearing out the warnings of those like Dr Hill who knew the Council's faith was misplaced. Except for the unpopular flats in Hospital and Palmer Streets, private builders conspicuously failed to provide the accommodation required by the poor. By 1913, this failure could be ignored no longer. A special Housing Inquiry Committee was appointed, chaired by Neville Chamberlain. Though loathe to spend public money on building houses, it realised that the council had to be involved deeply in development. Its recommendations reflected this dualistic approach. The council was advised to buy estates and develop them for house building on town-planning lines with space for public buildings, recreation grounds, and allotments; and to construct roads and lay on gas, water, and electricity mains. Yet, it should retain the freehold of building plots, leasing them on low ground rents to private builders who would erect houses subject to restrictions on numbers, character and rental. The council was increasing its commitment to development. It seemed only a matter of time before the need for council houses was recognised.

27

The Housing Inquiry Committee had the misfortune to tackle the accumulated housing problems caused by 100 years of inaction. Progressive councils highlighted the inertia of nineteenth century Birmingham. Manchester had banned back-to-backs in 1844, and from 1869 Liverpool embarked on a policy of slum clearance and municipal house building. By 1912, an active Conservative council there had improved over 11,000 houses, demolished 5,500 and built 2,322 properties. The contrast with Birmingham was glaring. Up to 1913, landlords had reconditioned 3,311 houses, 2,774 had been knocked down, and a meagre 165 council homes built in their place. Slum-patching cost little to the ratepayers only, 15s a head compared with £56 a head for Liverpool's policy, but it could only be a stop-gap measure. The long-term deterioration of back-to-back housing was not halted, but a decisive solution to the housing question was prevented, and a higher cost ensured when a resolute approach was agreed. The Committee recognised that the council had 'merely played' with the housing problem by building a few houses in Milk Street. Successful municipal housing had to be large scale, but this was a daunting outlook. Birmingham had 43,366 back-to-backs; 42,020 houses without their own water supply; and 58,028 with no separate lavatory. Any rehousing scheme for those living in inadequate housing meant building at least 50,000 houses. Not surprisingly, this prospect was balked at because of the gigantic cost necessary. The declaration of war in 1914 stifled further discussion of the dilemma.

In weighing up the pros and cons of municipal housing, one thing must be kept clearly in mind. To be successful it must be carried out on a large scale.

(Special Housing Inquiry Report, 1914)

24, Bullock Street, one of Birmingham's first travellers' sites; about 1905. (Birmingham Library Services)

It is found that the herding together of large masses of people in cheerless houses, without a chance of ready access to natural beauties, affects the occupants in a profound and far-reaching manner. Thriftlessness, intemperance, and a number of vices are fostered by such surroundings.

(Dr Robertson, Annual Report, Medical Officer of Health, 1906)

Courtyard in Summer Lane, early 1920s. Notice the large number of children - one in the front row is barefooted and most of the rest are wearing Daily Mail charity boots.
(Birmingham Library Services)

Before 1914, the housing question was not just a matter of improving the living conditions of the poor because it was the right and humane thing to do. For many middle-class people, housing was inextricable from morality. They assumed that bad housing fostered bad behaviour. In their misguided opinion, poorer people were more prone to drunkenness, violence, over-spending and sexual immorality just because they lived in back-to-back houses. The crowding of people in the congested central wards of Birmingham and other big cities was believed to lead to the triumph of the beast in people. Consequently, housing must be improved if the morals of the poor were to be raised. There was a strong admixture of self-interest and self preservation in this argument of the rich. They feared the poor. By the 1900s the middle class birth rate had declined sharply whilst that of the poor stayed high: in 1905, in the deprived ward of Deritend, it was 34.9, but in Edgbaston it was only 19.7. It was thought that the growing numbers of the poor were a danger to the ruling class. Further, because they were malnourished, they tended to be smaller in physique and were not regarded as good workers or soldiers. Better houses were needed, then, not only for the well-being of the poor: the preservation of the social order and of the Empire demanded that they should be well-housed.

The poor lived hidden away from the prosperous. Their narrow streets and labyrinthine courtyards seemed forbidding and unwelcoming. The middle class feared them as unknown territories, sending missionaries to establish mission halls and civilise their inhabitants. Little did they realise that the poor could have taught them much about sharing, helping the needy, and caring for others. Of course, poorer districts had their quota of unkind and dislikeable people, but so too did middle-class areas. Poverty and bad housing did not make the poor inhuman, instead it made them more aware of the needs of each other. Life in a poor locality would have been unbearable without good neighbourliness. Each neighbourhood seemed to have a local `mother' to whom everyone would run for advice if there was sickness or an accident. Poverty meant little money for doctors or undertakers, so other women delivered babies and laid out the dead - at no cost. Communal support was everywhere in a poor neighbourhood - from minding children and granny rearing to lending food and giving sympathy. Pawnbrokers were often friendly, lending more money than an article was worth, and corner shopkeepers threw out a valuable life line with strap. Poverty-stricken neighbourhoods were not slumped in despair - there was friendship as well as dislike, laughter as well as sadness. To outsiders they were inhospitable and ought to be erased; to those who belonged, they provided support and made life bearable.

One wonders today how we can say they were happy days, but they were, we had never known luxury, so it wasn't missed or craved for, it was the small things in life, the togetherness, and love from family life. (Mrs Muckler, Stoke Street, Ladywood)

Courtyard in Cromwell Street, Nechells, about 1905 - redeveloped in the 1950s for the Bloomsbury Estate. Notice the matriarchal woman in the foreground: her front yard surrounded by the only fence in the court; a washing line stretching from her wall; and plants outside her windowsill. Obviously the yard's 'gaffer'. (Birmingham Library Services)

Chapter 2: The Era of Council Housing

To let them (our heroes) come home from horrible, water-logged trenches to something little better than a pigsty here would, indeed, be criminal . . . and a negation of all we have said during the war, that we can never repay those men for what they have done for us.

(Walter Long, President of the Local Government Board, in Richard Reiss, The Home I Want, 1918)

Soldiers, wounded in The First World War, at convalescence; about 1915. Richard Chinn, Coldstream Guardsman and Old Contemptible, in wheelchair.
(Stella Couper)

The First World War had a tremendous effect on attitudes towards the housing problem. Britain's rulers and prosperous classes had been amazed at the patriotism of the working class. Men and women had volunteered in their hundreds of thousands to fight and work for a country which had failed the poor; which had given them poverty rather than comfort, ill-health instead of vitality, slum housing in place of decent homes. The realisation dawned that the poor were not a separate race, that they were as much British as were the middle class. Their efforts in contributing to victory had to be recognised and rewarded, and an unwritten social contract evolved. The sacrifice of the people was to be matched by a government commitment to major social reforms once the war was ended. Expectations were raised that women would be given the vote, that there would be educational reform, the extension of national insurance, and much else. But the greatest hopes were attached to a solution to the housing problem. Lloyd George, the Prime Minister, and his cabinet recognised that this was the crux of any social reform. They began to plan a housing policy which was to be started once Germany was defeated. It was symbolised by the slogan, 'Homes Fit for Heroes', which swept the land and was taken up by the working class with fervour and eagerness.

Before 1914, housing reformers were motivated by a genuine concern for the distress of the poor, and by a fear that they threatened the social order. For many, better housing was a humanitarian gesture but it was also practical as it would lead to fitter and less discontented workers. Despite the increased emphasis on social concern after 1919, this element of expediency did not disappear from the housing question. During the last year of the war, 41% of conscripts were medically graded as unfit for military service. The future of the nation was believed to be dependent on raising these men, classified as C.3, in to the A.1. category of fitness and strength. Decent housing, it was felt, would do this, as well as avoid unrest and improve the 'morals' of the poor. Justness and political judgement, then, made the government aware that urgent action was needed if the housing problem was not to lead to graver social problems. But heroes were returning to even more depressing conditions than they had left. In Birmingham, an investigation revealed that out of 600 discharged soldiers with tuberculosis, no less than 107 were living in dwellings containing two families. Thus, men with an infective disease were sleeping in the same room as their wives and children. The housing problem keenly affected many people; it demanded a drastic solution.

If a healthy race is to be reared, it can only be reared in healthy homes; if drink and crime are to be success-fully combated, decent, sanitary houses must be provided; if 'unrest' is to be converted into contentment, the provision of good houses may prove to be one of the most potent agents in that conversion.

(George V, The Times, 1919)

Susan & Hyram Flint and children in the garden of no. 6 back of 75, Bromsgrove Street - a 3-storey back-to-back; early 1920s. Despite the belief of some, the poor were no less human than the better off - they were just poorer. (Mrs A Mansell)

Before the war municipal house-building had been rejected as too socialistic. It was now seen to be the only solution.

(When We Build Again, 1941)

Corner of Kenwood Road, Batchelor's Farm Estate, Bordesley Green, 1926; 1,360 houses were built here at one of Birmingham's first inter-war council estates. (Birmingham Library Services)

Whatever its source, the recognition grew that both the state and councils had to be involved actively in solving the housing problem. A decisive shift in attitudes was signified firstly by the formation of an Advisory Housing Panel, and secondly by a government appeal issued to local authorities in 1917. This made the point that private enterprise would be unable to deal swiftly and successfully with the massive house-building programme which was needed once peace came. By 1918 the wind of change resulted in a momentous transformation of policy. The government agreed to offer substantial financial aid to councils which would undertake municipal house-building, and it accepted the revolutionary recommendations of the Tudor Walters Committee on Working-Class Housing. Building was to be encouraged, but at no more than twelve houses per acre in towns. A minimum of 70 feet should separate opposing houses, so that there could be a proper penetration of light in the winter. Eight was to be the maximum number of dwellings in a block; different styles of housing in the same road were advocated; and wide frontages were advised so as to prevent the construction of narrow but deep, tunnel-back houses. Consequently, long, dreary, parallel terraces were discouraged. Most importantly, the committee believed it essential that each house should have at least a living room, parlour and scullery downstairs, three bedrooms above, and a larder and bathroom. Brighter, more airy, and larger homes were offered as a prospect to the working class. The era of municipal house-building was at hand.

Britain's coalition government had assented to the far-reaching and visionary recommendations of the Tudor Walters Report. However, if its advice was to be acted on and the housing problem tackled determinedly, then effective legislation was required speedily. This came with the Housing and Town Planning Act of 1919, also known as the Addison Act after the minister who supervised its introduction. Previous to the First World War, many of the provisions of housing acts were not compulsory, councils implemented them only if they wished to. The Addison Act ended this age of permissive housing legislation, whilst heralding the new policy of municipal house-building aided by the state. For the first time a national act placed on local authorities the responsibility of providing adequate housing for working-class people. Councils were required to find out the need for working-class dwellings in their areas and to make plans to provide for it which were to be approved by the Ministry of Health. The government offered financial assistance to limit any losses made by councils in excess of a penny rate, thus introducing the principle of support from the state. The better structure and superior amenities planned for the new council houses meant that an economic rent would have placed them beyond the reach of the people they were designed for. Consequently, another significant principle established was that of fixing their rents independently of costs for their building.

. . . the whole object of the Housing and Town Planning Bill of 1919 is to cause a rapid provision of a large number of houses of a character far superior to the majority of houses now occupied by the working classes. (Sir John Robertson, Housing and Public Health, 1919)

Court no. 7, Pershore Street, mid 1920s; notice the maiding tub in front of the brew 'us - adjoining the communal toilets - and the woman pegging out. (Sylvia Leigh)

In my opinion there is only one remedy, viz., the replacement of these slums by decent houses in a pleasant environment.

(Dr Robertson, Annual Report, Medical Officer of Health, 1918)

No. 10 Court, Hurst Street, mid-1920s; notice the 'miskins' (dustbins) and the baby playing in the background. Of Birmingham's huge number of nineteenth-century back-to-backs only a few remain today, four of them at the corner of Inge & Hurst Streets.
(Sylvia Leigh)

On a local level, Birmingham reflected the seriousness of the housing problem which had led to fundamental shifts in government policy. The city's normal building requirement was 2,500 new houses each year, but construction had stopped during the war. Consequently, by 1918 there was a pressing housing shortage in Birmingham, exacerbated by a rise in population because of a war-time influx of workers. Over 12,000 dwellings had to be built immediately to catch up with the back log, and this was without attention to the formidable problems posed by the increasingly dilapidated back-to-backs of the city. Many had been condemned before the war and more had become unfit to live in because they had not been repaired or decorated since 1914. Nearly 200,000 people lived in them - a population as large as Cardiff or Bolton - and the detrimental effect they had on health was illustrated graphically in 1918 by Dr Robertson. He showed that those parts of Birmingham where back-to-backs were most common were the areas where the death rates were at their highest for diarrhoea, measles, bronchitis and pneumonia, and phthisis (wasting disease). They were also the worst districts for infant mortality and their general death rate was twice as high as that of suburban wards. The grimness of the housing situation was realised by the council. In 1917 a new Housing and Town Planning Committee was established and the following year it accepted the government's scheme of encouraging municipal building. It became obvious that the answer to the housing problem was to be found in a partnership between local and national authorities.

In 1917 the council's Public Health Committee had called the attention of the Housing Committee to the depressing contrast between the health of the people of the various areas of Birmingham. The opinion was held that the high sickness and mortality rates in the central wards called for a radical improvement in the housing conditions of those districts. However, because of the housing shortage in the city, the measures needed to remedy the problem could not be taken until there was a considerable addition made to the number of working-class dwellings. The Housing Committee was requested earnestly to give the subject their earliest possible consideration, but it was not until the passing of the Addison Act that a coherent and effective housing policy could be contemplated. Consequently, Birmingham council set up a Housing and Estates Department with a regular committee and a Housing Director as a full-time official. His brief was to plan and supervise the building of municipal estates; to manage them; and to collect the rents. However, his job was made burdensome by severe post-war difficulties. There were shortages of materials and of labour - especially bricklayers - and there was controversy over the employment of private contractors, instead of direct labour, to build council houses. Still, it was hoped that a vigorous programme of rehousing in the suburbs would solve the problems of the central wards.

I am convinced that housing is at the root of many of our gravest social problems, and that more can be done for the good of the City by a proper solution of this question than by any other course of action which lies open to the city council.

(George Cadbury, Memorandum on the Housing Problem in Birmingham etc., 1918)

No. 7 Court William Street, about 1905; the unplanned mixture of 2 and 3 storey back-to-backs in this photograph indicates the haphazard growth of central Birmingham. Notice, too, the women peeling potatoes in the yard, the nets on the windows and the plants on the outside window sills. (Birmingham Library Services)

Various estimates have been given as to the number of people from the central areas who need to be re-housed. It may be said, however, that during the next twenty years, on a moderate computation, at least 50,000 houses should be dealt with . . .

(Housing and Town Planning Committee, Report, 1918)

Newly-built council housing at Cotterills Lane, Stechford; mid 1920s .
(Birmingham Library Services)

The new Housing Manager was faced with a severe crisis. Birmingham's population had increased, new building had ceased, and there were around 40,000 back-to-backs needing to be cleared and their tenants rehoused. 5,000 homes had to be built each year for the next twenty years if the city's housing problem was to be tackled successfully. Despite difficulties with labour and materials a start was made quickly on providing the new council dwellings needed so desperately. By the end of 1919 tenants moved in to the corporation houses in Cotterills Lane, Alum Rock - the first occupied under the new building programme. Other dwellings were built at Billesley Farm, Pineapple Farm (Kings Heath) Stonehouse Farm (California), and elsewhere. In all, 3,234 houses were erected under the 1919 scheme. All were of a good construction and in terms of space they were the best built by the council between the wars. They were fitted with dressers and cupboards; supplied with gas lighting; and had a separate bathroom. Nearly 3,000 were of the 3B type, having a living room, parlour, scullery, and three bedrooms. Unlike much council housing later, this design reflected the wishes of prospective tenants. It was based on the recommendations of the Tudor Walters Report which had listened to groups like the Women's Labour League. These had indicated the preference of working-class people for a parlour and living room rather than a through lounge.

By 1922, the council had erected houses in Birchfield, Bordesley Green, Bournville, California, Erdington, Gospel Oak, Kings Heath, Little Bromwich, Quinton, Short Heath, Stechford, and Warstock. Rapidly, agricultural land was transformed into residential areas, and the Housing and Estates Department decided their new tenants needed advice on maintaining their homes and estates in a respectable fashion. With funds from the Common Good Trust, the Municipal Tenants Monthly was launched. It encouraged gardening on council estates, distributed useful information to tenants, and tried to foster a spirit of neighbourliness amongst them. Their efforts were well-intentioned but artificial, and the magazine was short-lived. Yet tenants recognised the need for communal action on estates where the housing was good but where facilities were lacking. Various associations were formed - like that for gardening on the Linden Road Estate - and the tenants' association on the Pineapple Estate. This aimed to protect tenants' interests; to co-operatively buy seeds and plants; to hire out gardening tools and books; to arrange lectures; and to pass on complaints to the Housing Department. Its representations led to the erection of a letter box and a public telephone box on the estate; and its actions indicated the importance of tenants pressure to establish essential facilities.

When I first visited the district in October 1920 . . . the difficulty was to find the Electors, in many cases there was a half a mile or more between the houses . . . the most striking fact is the remarkable change which has come over Billesley and Yardley Wood. In place of hundreds of acres of agriculture land and half-a-dozen farms the area is now covered by more than two thousand houses.

(Councillor Griffin, The Billesley Tenants Association Magazine 1926)

The development of the Warren Farm and Kingstanding Council Estates, 1929.
(Birmingham Library Services)

Instead, we found ourselves in modern houses, with hot and cold water laid on (many houses in this country have not even the latter!) with large gardens awaiting cultivation, and then full of promise of reward. We found conveniences for coal storage in the dry, without cartage through the house; we found back and front entrances installed; suitable washing and bathroom accommodation was a fully appreciated point; not to mention the airing cupboard upstairs. Then, did we appreciate burglar-proof non-falling windows, or mice-proof cement halls and kitchens, design of structure for gas stove? Ah!

("Jud", Municipal Tenants Monthly, 1922)

Municipal dwellings at Arkley Road, Gospel Oak; mid 1930s.
(Birmingham City Council Housing Department)

As our garden was a field only nine months ago, there are many ways in which I can help Daddy. The ground is full of stones; so these have to be dug out, and be placed on the path where Daddy will dig them in. Then I can keep off the edge of the lawn until it is properly set. I can keep the tools clean and oiled; and when Daddy wants them, get them out; and put them back when finished with. When Daddy was making the arches over the path, I held the branches for him. Whenever I see manure on the road, I get it for the marrow bed. Then there are seeds to plant; while Daddy makes the holes, I hold, and put into the holes, potatoes, etc. We also have a bird-table where waste scraps and crumbs are put; this I keep supplied. (Herbert Wallace Litten, age 12 years, Brook Lane, Kings Heath, Municipal Tenants Monthly, 1922).

Originally, Birmingham council had intended to erect 10,000 houses under the 1919 Act, but its construction programme was beset by problems and it failed to reach its target by nearly 6,000 dwellings. A major reason for this shortfall was the soaring cost of building nationally which led to an average price of £1,000 for Addison houses. Those built in Birmingham cost between £900 and £1,000 each - about four times the pre-war level. Spiralling expenses were not unique to the city. The unlimited government subsidy beyond the figure of a penny rate encouraged profiteering by some builders and extravagance by some local authorities. As the brief post-war boom turned swiftly in to depression, the government decided that no longer could it afford to subsidise municipal house-building. In 1921 construction costs reached their climax and this provided the opportunity for the state to limit its liability. The Addison Act fell victim to the notorious `Geddes Axe' which stopped all new approvals for building programmes. This resulted in a significant slowing down in the construction activities of local authorities. Runaway expenditure came at an opportune time for those who opposed public involvement in the provision of homes for working-class people. Many expressed the hope that the building industry would return to its pre-war economic basis. This meant a withdrawal of involvement by the state and a reliance on private enterprise to supply the housing needs of newly-weds and slum dwellers.

Isn't the demand of the newly-married for a separate house a comparatively modern development? In China and the East generally, I understand, they continue to live under the parental roof quite contentedly.

(Alfred Mond, Minister of Health, in, Christopher Addison, The Betrayal of the Slums, 1922)

The wedding of Marjory & Fred Luckett of Aston; late 1920s. (Arthur Wilkes)

The history of the housing question in Birmingham is a troubled and chequered one, as full of changes as the kaleidoscope of life.

(Birmingham Evening Mail, 1922)

The development of the Pineapple Farm Estate; 1921.
(Birmingham Weekly Post)

Once again, the national debate on the housing question was mirrored in Birmingham. From its inception in 1919, critics had attacked the Housing and Town Planning Committee as slow, inefficient, wasteful and ill-advised. Controversy over its activities increased, and although from November 1919 it had a preponderance of Labour councillors, the disapproval of the committee's activities was not fully a political issue. Its first chairman, George Cadbury, was a Liberal, and he was followed by Siward James, a Conservative. Indeed, the highly censorious Evening Mail emphasised that reactions against the committee should not be regarded as demonstrations against Labour Party ideals or methods. Eventually, the storm of censure led the council to set up a Special Committee of Inquiry in to the workings of the Housing Committee. Its report, published in 1922, was highly critical of inexperienced officials, of the lack of careful supervision of housing contracts, of friction with builders, and of ill-feeling with the Public Works Committee which was responsible for roads and drainage works. With hindsight, much of the condemnation seems unfair. The Ministry of Health was urging councils to build good quality houses, Birmingham had a severe housing problem, and exorbitant building prices were a national difficulty. The most relevant criticism was of the unwise purchase of estates which were distant from the city, and without roads or drainage. Consequently, they were costly to develop and this increased expense led to the building of fewer houses than planned.

Following the adverse report on its activities, in April 1922 the Housing Committee put forward a statement as to its future policy. 1,800 houses had been built up to that date, but the committee still had on its books 10,000 applicants and believed it would have more if people had any hope of obtaining a home. Consequently, it wanted to make representations to the Ministry of Health to build more dwellings under the assisted houses scheme, bringing them up to a total of 6,000. However, the sustained assault on its actions since 1919 took its toll. The hostile publicity continued, three members of the Housing Committee resigned, and it was felt by many councillors that insufficient attention had been taken of the charges laid against it. Alderman Sir David Brooks had headed the Special Inquiry Committee, and he proposed that there would be a more speedy and economical building of houses if the responsibility for construction under the state-assisted scheme be transferred from the Housing and Estates Committee. After a long and animated debate this proposal was carried by 53 votes to 34. As a result, the newly-named Public Works and Town Planning Committee became responsible for building council houses, whilst an Estates Committee became responsible for the management of corporation estates and for the allocation of houses on them to applicants.

When the Housing Committee began to break up, when its members began to show that they could not even work in harmony with one another and present a solid front to a highly critical Council and public, its position became impossible. The time had come for drastic change. (Birmingham Post, 1922)

The Estates Department, Summer Lane, 1933. On display are prize-winners from the council's popular gardening competitions.
(Birmingham City Council Housing Department)

Private housing at Princethorpe Road, Weoley Castle, mid 1930s.
(Bournville Village Trust)

Opponents of the Housing Committee declared that they were not against council house-building, but their victory did echo the national resurgence of support for private builders. The Public Works Committee was in favour of private enterprise whenever possible, a feeling shared by the Conservative minister responsible for housing policy, Neville Chamberlain, M.P. for Birmingham Ladywood. His solution to the national housing problem imitated the city's long-held faith in the private sector as the agent of housing reform. Accordingly, the 1923 Housing Act aimed to stimulate private development, revive the building trade and accelerate the erection of dwellings. Councils were encouraged to lend money to enable private purchase of homes, building societies were supported in making mortgages easier, and a subsidy was provided for both dwellings built by local authorities and private builders. However, an annual grant of £6 per house for twenty years was the most councils could claim, and they could only build if the Minister was convinced that it would be better for them to do so than private enterprise. As a result of a general fall in prices, and because of the sudden reduction in demand for building after the 'Geddes Axe', construction costs fell sharply to about half their previous level. Yet, the new subsidy was not large enough to revive municipal house-building on a large scale. Those living in insanitary dwellings still awaited an extensive housing programme to improve their lives.

The policy of encouraging local authorities to become the main providers of houses for working-class people suffered a complete reversal with Chamberlain's Act of 1923. However, it invigorated the private sector. In Birmingham private builders had erected only 382 houses in 1922; by 1924 this annual figure had risen to 1,201. Undoubtedly, their renewed interest was stimulated by the council's decision to pass on in a lump sum of £75 the grant provided by the Act. The city itself added another £25, giving a total subsidy to private builders of £100 per house. This was subject to a maximum selling price of £600 freehold, exclusive of the subsidy. In 1927 a reduction in the annual government grant led the council to drop its lump sum subsidy to £50, and the following year the scheme ended when the state abandoned the grant altogether. Not only was the council influential in lowering the price of houses built by private enterprise, it also instituted a progressive mortgage scheme. This helped people who wished to build dwellings by granting them loans on advantageous terms. The amount advanced represented about 90% of the value of the house when completed, payable in instalments as the building proceeded; and the scheme terminated in 1931 after the building of 1,377 dwellings. Average three-bedroom houses without a parlour had fallen in cost from £930 in August 1920, to £436 in March 1922. This drop and the availability of easier mortgages from 1923, enabled a few highly-paid members of the working class to buy their own homes. Nevertheless, home-buying remained unattainable for the vast majority of working-class families.

. . . there can be no immediate solution of the Housing problem except through private enterprise.

(Public Works and Town Planning Committee, Report, 1922)

Private building at the edge of the Green Belt, 1930s. (Bournville Village Trust)

MUNICIPALITY PROVIDES HOMES ON HIRE PURCHASE.   TRAIN

One of the sixteen happy families in Birmingham Corporation's novel ready-made flat homes at Hay Mill, where the tenants this week experience the last payment feeling in ending the 3s. per week instalments for the furniture supplied by the Corporation three years ago, to enable young married couples to obtain their own homes. This is the first time a municipality has conducted such an experiment.

Homes in Hay Mills furnished with a hire-purchase scheme run by the council; 1930.
(Birmingham Weekly Post)

To try and extend home ownership to the working class, the council introduced an exciting scheme enabling corporation tenants to buy their property. The subsidy under Chamberlain's Act was passed on to the purchaser; mortgages were provided by the Birmingham Municipal Bank; and the Estates Department handled sales, publishing a booklet in 1925 called, How to be Your Own Landlord. It divided the city in to five districts, though no municipal houses were for sale in the central area. Corporation dwellings built specifically for purchase were available in Acocks Green, Alum Rock, Bordesley Green, Billesley, Erdington, Fox Hollies, Hay Mills, Kings Heath, Pype Hayes, Short Heath, Small Heath and Ward End. By 1929, when the subsidy was discontinued, more than £1,000,000 had been loaned by the Municipal Bank to buyers of 3,314 council houses. In 1925 an end or semi-detached parlour-type home in Foxton Road, Alum Rock, cost £468, with £448 for a middle house. An end or semi-detached non parlour-type house in Brookvale Park Road, Erdington, cost £338, with £317 for a middle house. Although the house purchasing scheme was adventurous and innovative, home ownership remained a daunting prospect. A house in Ilford Road, Short Heath cost £372 to buy in 1925, plus £3. 6s legal fees. If a £20 deposit was paid and £352 borrowed over twenty years at 5% interest, the tenant needed to find 13s weekly in repayments, plus 6s for rates, ground rent and insurance. This compared to an inclusive council rent of 11s 2d - and even this was still a fifth of an average working man's wage.

Unsurprisingly, a Conservative government had encouraged home ownership. Easier mortgages, government subsidies and falling building costs allowed many lower-middle-class people to buy their own houses for the first time. In Birmingham, the local Conservative party was reliant on widespread working-class support for its council majority and so it was more sensitive than the national party to the needs of upper-working class families. Consequently, it had made a determined attempt to enable them to buy their properties. Yet, neither private purchase nor council house-building catered for most working class people, let alone the huge numbers of the poor living in back-to-backs. The Public Works Committee acknowledged this, and though staunchly in favour of private enterprise, it confessed that at least in the short term, the council had to build as many houses as possible. In 1922 it reported that the 1919 Act had not solved the city's housing problem. Indeed, at just over a third of the annual average before 1906, house-building was not even providing for Birmingham's normal growth in population. Furthermore, the rent of municipal dwellings was too dear for the average working-class family, let alone the poor. This damning indictment of national housing policy led the council to instruct the Committee to erect as many houses as possible in the next two years - even without government approval or financial assistance; and to acquire and develop building estates subject to a financial loss of no more than a 3d rate.

Moreover, the question of erecting houses for occupation by people who live in slum areas, whose houses will have to be dealt with under slum clearance schemes, has not been met in any way whatever.
(Public Works and Town Planning Committee, Report, 1922)

A matriarchal figure striding towards the camera at 6, Bell Barn Road; 1934. Notice, too, the clean washing and the advertisements for Wills' cigarettes. (Sylvia Leigh)

Ted Reynolds as a child outside his family's council house at 4, Eastlands Road, Moseley; about 1927.
(Mr Reynolds)

The Public Works and Town Planning Committee had an avowed preference for private enterprise. It recognised that the smaller type of villa built for sale would help the lower middle class directly, but it argued that indirectly the working class would benefit. This would be achieved by a filtering up process. Home buyers would vacate their rented accommodation which then would be occupied by the better-paid of the working class. In turn, their former houses would be rented by the poor, leaving the back-to-backs of the city abandoned. In this way, all Brummies would naturally and easily move in to better housing. This policy took little account of the inability of the poor to afford to rent dwellings other than back-to-backs, nor did it pay attention to their need to live near the available work, and it ignored the pull of communal loyalty and neighbourhood support. Utopian in thought and practice, it could never have solved Birmingham's housing problem and as such it gave way to harsh reality. To its credit, the committee ditched its principles, recognising that it was of outstanding importance for the council to build small houses. Indeed, in 1923 it erected 1,508 dwellings, whereas 970 had been the highest annual total built under the Housing and Town Planning Committee. Still, this rate of building was not enough. By 1925 it was estimated that there was a shortage of 30,000 dwellings in Birmingham; there were 24,840 applicants for new housing registered with the Estates Department; and overcrowding had increased in poorer areas. Many more new houses were needed desperately. They could be provided only if central government assisted councils with subsidies.

47

By the mid-twenties the shortage of working-class houses was greater than in 1919, when the boast of `Homes Fit for Heroes' had seemed set to eradicate slum property. In 1924 the first Labour government came to power and it was determined to tackle this housing crisis. Wheatley, the new Minister of Health, introduced a Housing Act and once more the balance tilted in favour of municipal building as the most effective response to the housing problem. The subsidy on new dwellings was increased to £9 per house for 40 years - on condition that local authorities also made an annual grant of not more than £4.10s per house. Subsidised homes had to be let, not sold; the benefit of the subsidy was to be passed on to tenants by reducing rents; and local authorities were to build their houses to the same standards laid down in Chamberlain's Act. This had promoted the building of non-parlour type homes with a bathroom, a policy advocated by the Public Works and Town Planning Committee in 1922. Such homes were smaller than those with a parlour, but on average they cost £50 less to construct and so more could be built at a lower rent. Obviously, tenants preferred a larger house with a parlour, but their costliness prevented them being a realistic answer to the massive housing shortage. The only viable solution was the erection of large numbers of non-parlour homes, at no more than 12 houses per acre. Although the amount of subsidy varied between 1924 and 1933, the Wheatley Act was the catalyst which caused a huge expansion in council house-building.

The Wheatley Act . . . brought in a new era of municipal house-building. It made possible mass-building and rentals for tenants at the normal artisan's economic level.

(When We Build Again, 1941)

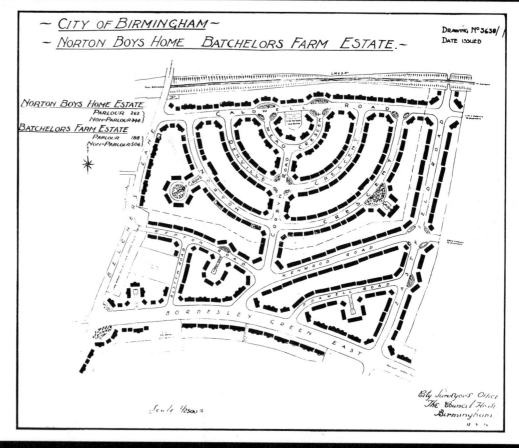

Plan of Batchelor's Farm Estate, Bordesley Green. The groves and crescents indicate the influence of town planners on the development of inter-war municipal estates. They show the rejection of the monotonous, Coronation-Street type roads of by-law housing favoured by private builders before 1914. (Birmingham Library Services)

BIRMINGHAM G

"ACHIEVEMENT WITHOUT PARALLEL"

CHANCELLOR PRAISES BIRMINGHAM

40,000 Houses

"AN achievement on the part of Birmingham which has no parallel in this or any other country."

In these words, the Chancellor of the Exchequer (Mr. Neville Chamberlain) summed up the city's record of municipal housing after he had opened Birmingham's 40,000th municipal house yesterday.

He was speaking to a large assembly of civic officials and others from a platform erected in the front garden of the house—No. 30, Hopstone-road, Weoley Castle Estate—and a few minutes before the Lord Mayor (Councillor H. E. Goodby) had proudly claimed that Birmingham City Council had housed 160,000 people —"almost a city in itself."

CASTLE CONTRAST

Later in the day, Mr. Chamberlain inspected the modern working-class houses on the Ashcroft Estate, which has arisen as the result of slum clearance in the Great Brook-street area; and, after opening the 40,000th house, he saw something of Birmingham's oldest "housing"—the newly-revealed remains of the centuries-old Weoley Castle, little more than a stone's throw away.

A commemorative cigar casket was presented to the Chancellor, who was afterwards a guest at a civic luncheon in the Council House.

At the luncheon Mr. Chamberlain referred to the "one weak spot in the otherwise satisfactory post-war history

Birmingham Gazette photograph.
At the inspection of Winson-street flats. Left to right: The Lord Mayor, Mr. H. H. Humphries and Mr. Chamberlain.

"BURGLARIOUS ENTRY"

A slight hitch in the opening of the 40,000th house provided a little comedy which robbed the occasion of some of its formality.

Mr. Chamberlain inserted the presentation key, turned it in the lock, and pushed the door—without result! The door resolutely refused to budge, in spite of the joint efforts of the Lord Mayor and the City Surveyor to turn the key. Finally, by giving it a hard push, two Public Works Department officials managed to open the door, which had become jammed at the top.

After inspecting the house, the Chancellor referred to the occasion as a "burglarious entry."

they would fill the need; and that if they could not or would not, "the Council must then again seriously consider the means of providing houses."

In a tribute to the work which Mr. Neville Chamberlain had done for the city and the State—"more houses were built in this country during the time that he was Minister of Health than at any other period of our national history"—the Lord Mayor pointed out that in a fortnight's time it will be 60 years since Mr. Joseph Chamberlain was first elected Mayor of Birmingham.

GRATEFUL CITY

"Birmingham is deeply grateful to the Chamberlain family," he added, "and the Birmingham City Council is, I am happy to say, still imbued with the Chamberlain tradition."

As a memento of the occasion, Mr. Chamberlain was presented by the chairman of the Public Works and Town Planning Committee (Councillor T. B. Hooper) with a cigar box. Acknowledging it, the Chancellor said: "I shall hold this wonderful present—and my children after me

Humphries (City Surveyor and Engineer) and Mrs. Humphries, Councillor T. B. Pritchett (chairman of the Estates Committee), Councillor H. Roberts (chairman of the Housing Committee), Mr. Wallace Smith (general manager of the Estates Dept.), Mr. W. H. Ballard (building surveyor), and Mr. H. H. Cope (clerk to the Estates Committee).

WAR MEMORY

The ceremony at the 40,000th house also found Mr. Chamberlain in reminiscent mood.

"I look back to-day," Mr. Chamberlain said, "to a time when I held the office of Lord Mayor of Birmingham and when I was addressing a meeting in the Town Hall.

"It was during the Great War, and I spoke with some emotion aroused by the thought that so many of our fellow

The opening of the 40,000th council house by Neville Chamberlain; 1933.
(Birmingham Gazette)

For 50 years Birmingham Council had believed that private enterprise would provide the answer to the city's dreadful housing problem. It was proven wrong. The realisation of this mistake came slowly, but once apparent the council enthusiastically adopted a programme of municipal house-building as encouraged by the Wheatley Act. The transformation in policy was astounding. In 1924, the year the act was passed, the city erected 1,663 houses; in 1925 this figure increased dramatically to 3,066. The same year the Birmingham Gazette reported that, on average, six houses per hour were being completed at the Batchelor's Farm Estate, Bordesley Green. In 1930 alone - the peak year of council house-building before 1939 - 6,715 corporation houses were erected. Indeed, on 25 July 1930, Arthur Greenwood - Labour's Minister of Health - opened Birmingham's 30,000th council house, in the appropriately-named Greenwood Place, Kingstanding. By 1933, when the Wheatley Act ceased operation, 33,612 corporation homes had been erected under its provisions, compared to only 3,433 under Chamberlain's Act. Birmingham had built more council houses than any other local authority in England. This success was due to a remarkable partnership between a Labour government and a Conservative led council, supported in its housing policy by Labour representatives. The depression of the 1930s led to a slowing down in council house-building, but in 1939 the 50,000th council house in the city was opened at Fellmeadow Road, Lea Hall. Rightly, Conservative and Labour councillors congratulated themselves on an achievement unique in the history of English local government.

49

The enlarged Birmingham of 1911 numbered 840,000 people; by 1931 the figure had increased considerably to 1,000,000. This overall rise disguised significant internal movements of population which indicated that a steady decentralisation was in process. Between 1921 and 1931 the number of people in the central wards of Birmingham declined from 242,000 to about 188,000 - a shrinkage of 22.5%. There was, too, a decrease in population in the middle ring wards, from 380,000 to around 288,000 - a drop of 24.1%. In contrast to these falls, was a huge increase in people living in the outer ring wards. Their population rose from 300,000 in 1921 to about 571,000 by 1931 - a massive 91% expansion. Obviously, a major factor in this phenomenal growth was the building of new council estates in districts which had joined the city in 1911 and afterwards. Not all the incorporated areas grew in numbers. Aston had much in common with the central wards of the old city - it was mostly built up, and many of its houses were back-to-backs; and, Handsworth, too, was largely developed. By comparison, although Erdington, Kings Norton, Northfield and Yardley were expanding rapidly, they contained farmland ripe for development. So too, did Quinton, Perry Barr - added to the city in 1928 - and Sheldon - included in 1931. It was in these districts that the majority of council estates were built in the inter-war years. Often, the only link they retained with their rural past was in their names - such as Glebe Farm, Gospel Farm and Billesley Farm.

'Squire' Mitchell, Shard End Farm, late 1920s.
(Birmingham Library Services)

. . . coming as they do from densely populated districts of none too salubrious nature . . . to new houses furnished with all modern conveniences and situated . . . within actual sight of rural surroundings, is nothing short of entering into a paradise on earth for the majority.
(Birmingham Evening Mail, 1930)

The planners of the new estates were determined that they should differ significantly from the middle ring wards developed by private enterprise before 1919. Here, miles of tunnel-back houses lined treeless, straight roads in a 'Coronation-Street' fashion. Areas like Small Heath and Sparkhill were an improvement on the dismal central wards, but they did not inspire enthusiasm in the supporters of the garden-city idea. The country-side had been banished from them, there were too many houses to the acre, and their long rows of terraced dwellings were regarded as soulless and monotonous. Birmingham's inter-war council estates reflected the distaste of town planner's for uniformity, but cost prevented them from emerging as ideal garden cities. They were characterised by a complex geometric pattern of straight roads, circles and crescents. Building was mostly twelve houses per acre, occasionally fifteen; houses were built in blocks of two, four or six - so breaking up frontage lines; and all had front and back gardens. Dwellings lay back 20 feet or more from tree lined roads, and they were interspersed by small, open sites. On the earlier large municipal estates, the houses varied little in design, but their layout was different and many natural features of the area were retained. As development progressed, the newer estates showed an improvement in architecture and site layout.

By-law housing in Oldfield Road, Sparkbrook, decorated for the silver jubilee of George V; 1935. Seated on the doorstep of her home at number 41 (far right) is Mrs Jessie Jones, just in front of her is Mrs Nellie Fisher with two friends from Woodfield Road, Mr Bednall (in cloth cap) and Mrs Kinsey.
(Mrs N E Jones, daughter-in-law of Jessie and daughter of Nellie Fisher)

Whatever the design of a council estate, there is little doubt that the provision of open spaces and the closeness to farm land were great attractions to working-class people. Children especially delighted in the fresh air and the freedom of wandering and playing in parks and the countryside. In the summer those living at Perry Common estate earned 6d a day helping with haymaking and potato picking. The contrast was stark with the older, treeless and grassless parts of Birmingham. In 1941 it was found that just over 1% of the area of the central wards was given over to parks or recreation grounds. This compared to nearly 5% in the middle ring and 8.5% in the outer ring. The National Playing Fields Association had suggested a standard of 6 acres of playing fields per 1,000 people - apart from parks and other open spaces. The ratio in the central wards was an appalling .2, rising to 1.6 in the middle ring and 5.8 in the outer ring. Gardens, too, were largely absent from the poorer parts of Birmingham - only a third of families had them compared to 96% in the new estates. Middle-class observers waxed lyrical about the sweet breeze from the Vale of Evesham blowing its uncontaminated fragrance over Billesley, giving health and vigour to its inhabitants. Though overstated, it is unlikely that working-class people would have disagreed too much with the sentiments.

. . . then we had the luck of moving to a "Brand New" "Council House" with a lovely garden back and front and plenty of fresh air. We were the first tenants in the road which was Kemberton Road, Weoley Castle. The back garden joined on to farm land where the cows used to come to the fence.

(Mrs Clift, Brearley Street, Aston and Weoley Castle)

Lawford Street Recreation Ground, 1928. Notice how the small playground is hemmed in by housing and how the younger children are minded by big brothers and sisters. (Birmingham Recreation and Community Services Department)

Council housing at Olton Boulevard East, Fox Hollies, 1930s. The large gardens and open spaces contrast with the cramped and overcrowded conditions in central Birmingham. (Bournville Village Trust)

In 1939, my parents arranged an exchange with someone who wanted to live in this area (Hockley) for some unknown reason, for a house on a wonderful new council estate at Perry Common. We therefore went to live at 24, Dovedale Road. It had a long garden, the bottom of which was a stream . . . and then there were beautiful open fields right up to Oscott College, and we could also see the observatory. I was not used to such open spaces, and my mother became very worried after a time, because I would not venture to the bottom of the garden, however, after a period of making friends and becoming used to the open spaces I was very happy indeed living there.

(Norman Fearn, Hockley and Perry Common)

I remember if you stood on tip-toe and looked in a certain direction you could just see the top of a tree.

(Mrs Woodfield, Bridge Street West, Hockley)

53

The accommodation of the new corporation homes was a distinct improvement on that which most tenants had been used to in privately-rented property. They were all fitted with dressers and cupboards, and after 1923 they were provided with electric lighting not gas. Each had a gas range, gas heating for the washing copper, and parlour-type homes had a hot water circulating system. Other less essential features added to the appeal of the houses - perhaps a mantlepiece over the fire place or picture rails around the walls. Under the Chamberlain and Wheatley Acts most of the municipal houses built were of the non-parlour variety - nearly 29,000 out of a total of almost 37,000. The majority of these had a hall, large living room, scullery, bathroom which opened out of the scullery, toilet, coal shed, larder and three bedrooms. There was a smaller non-parlour type which had similar accommodation but less floor area; and a version which had just two bedrooms. Even this was vastly better than a back-to-back which had no bathroom, washing copper or toilet, and which had only a living room, cellar, two bedrooms, and a tiny scullery containing a black iron stove and a brown crock sink. There was little romantic about fetching coal from a damp, unlighted cellar, or in washing in the brew 'us in the dark and cold of a winter's night.

We left Heathmill Lane when I was ten yrs old in 1939 when war was declared to live in Yardley Wood ... About 6 months before we moved in the previous tenant had the gas mantle taken out and electric installed. As you may know we were in a new world. The toilet was still outside but our own.
(Mrs Malyn, Heathmill Lane and Yardley Wood)

Alice Brooks with her children Billy & Sylvia in a courtyard in Bishop Street, about 1935; a maid (dolly) can be seen behind them in the brew 'us.
(Mrs Beryl Brooks)

Women mangling washing outside the brew 'us, no. 12 Court, Cecil Street, mid 1930s.
(Sylvia Leigh)

At the top of the yard in Barker Street where we lived were two houses facing the entry into the street. In between the two houses was the wash house or 'brew 'us' where the women did their washing. They kept to their own side, one wringer or 'mangle' on one wall and the other opposite. There was no 'free for all', every family kept to their own limits.

(Mrs Piper, Barker Street, Ladywood)

Wash day was usually on a Monday which was done in the brewhouse up the yard where wood and coal were used to boil up water for the washing. It was my job to start the fire and fill the boiler. I have watched my mother scrubbing collars and boiler suits till 10 o'clock at night. She used to take in washing for other people who paid her about 1s 9d a bundle . .

(Mrs Scott, Carver Street, Hockley)

Commentators were fulsome in their praise of the new council estates. They were cleaner, brighter and closer to the country than the central and middle wards; the houses were better-built and equipped with 'up-to-date' facilities; and they possessed gardens encouraging tenants to grow flowers and vegetables. Certainly, these features were appreciated by working-class people, but increasingly they realised that there was a lack of facilities on the new estates. In 1932 a comparison was made between Kingstanding, with about 30,000 people, and the slightly smaller Shrewsbury. The older Shropshire town had 30 churches, fifteen church halls and parish rooms, five other halls, two public libraries, four picture houses and 159 public houses. Kingstanding was a glaring contrast in the provision of communal services. It boasted only one church, one hall, one picture house and one pub, and no parks, sports grounds, or hospital. An experimental community centre was planned by the council in 1930, but it was abandoned because of a financial crisis. Consequently, local people organised their own, opening the Perrystanding Community Centre off Kingstanding Circle in 1932. Soon after a sports' ground in Cooksey Lane was acquired, and in 1934 a branch of the Summer Lane Settlement was opened. On other estates it was a similar story. At Witton Lodge a Salvation Army building was used as a centre, and at Gospel Oak a charity had erected a community hall. It was not until 1936 that Birmingham's first council-funded community centre opened in Billesley, at the junction of Trittiford and Chinnbrook Roads.

It was awfully cold at Kingstanding in the winter, it was called Little Russia, and it was said that if you could live there you could live anywhere. The house was a non parlour council house and I think the rent was about 10/- (ten shillings).

(Hilda Hughes, Aston & Kingstanding)

Party at Firbeck Grove, Kingstanding, celebrating the silver jubilee of George V, 1935.
(Mrs Hemming)

From smoke to fresh air, from everlasting noise to peace and the song of birds, from drudgery to leisure and then . . . what?

(Birmingham Council for Community Associations, 1936)

Trittiford Road Junior School, 1932. (Billesley School)

Inevitably, the rapid development of council estates meant that the building of houses outran the provision of facilities for the new population. Tenants' associations, the council and charitable organisations made serious attempts to provide for the deficiency of telephone boxes, libraries, banks, and much else. In particular the need for community halls was addressed by the Birmingham Council for Community Associations for the New Housing Estates. Yet by 1936, when 1 in 6 Brummies lived in these areas, only five estates had a community hall - Allen's Cross, Billesley, Glebe Farm, Kingstanding and Weoley Castle. The provision of schools also lagged behind the erection of houses and a burgeoning population. Development at Billesley had begun in 1919, but not until 1925 was a school opened in Trittiford Road. Even then it was insufficient for the number of children in the district - it was built for 400 children but 600 were in attendance. An extension was planned to open in October 1926, giving an extra 400 places, but fifteen to twenty families were moving in to the locality each week. So great was the number of children waiting to join the school that it could only take those aged between five and nine. Older children would still have to attend a school outside the district - most travelling to Colmore Road in Kings Heath, or Dennis Road in Balsall Heath. Naturally, parents were annoyed at what seemed a lack of co-ordination between the Estates Committee, which managed the estate, and the Education Committee, which provided schools. Much of this disjunction between departments was unavoidable, but it rankled nevertheless.

Despite the importance of community centres and schools, they were not the most pressing need for many council tenants. They identified quick and cheap transport to and from the city as an urgent priority. At three miles distance, Batchelor's Farm was the nearest estate to town, whilst Allen's Cross, Kingstanding and Lea Hall were five miles away. Although Pype Hayes adjoined an industrial area, few estates had any significant local employment. The huge Stechford Ward included the Lea Hall and Glebe Farm estates, but in 1938 it provided work for only two out of three of its inhabitants. In contrast, the central wards contained only a fifth of Birmingham's population but provided work for over a third. Accordingly, many workers had to make dear and lengthy journeys to their jobs. It cost 10d and took nearly an hour for a return journey to town from Kingstanding, and from Allen's Cross two buses had to be caught. The Billesley Tenants' Association cited the case of a family rehoused in the district after their home in Aston was condemned. Previously, three of its members had walked to their jobs in Erdington, but now they each had to travel six or seven miles at the cost, between them, of 21s a week. Unsurprisingly, they wished they were back in Aston, even if it were in a dilapidated house. The association campaigned strongly for a direct bus route to the city centre, and for workmen's fares, their anger heightened by the swiftness of providing a bus service for Handsworth Wood. Eventually, the campaign was successful late in 1925.

When will the Corporation of Birmingham realise that they are in duty bound to provide through their Tramways Department quick and cheap facilities for their tenants in Billesley?
(The Billesley Tenants Association Magazine, 1925)

Emily Street viewed from Dymock Street, early 1930s. This area was typical of the central wards in its abundance of pubs and corner shops, and in its proximity to factories and workshops. (Sylvia Leigh)

Last day of service of trams on the Stechford route, 2 December 1948.
(Mr L. W. Perkins)

THE BILLESLEY BUS SERVICE

Attend all folks who in Billesley dwell,
Whilst I of the bus service do tell.
You who breathe sweet breezes from Evesham's Vale,
And feel the force of the south west gale.

You all remember the time, do you not?
When the roads were rough and a dirty lot.
No buses to carry you near or far,
And you had to walk and your pleasure to mar.

All the kiddies had a terrible time,
Through the rain, and the mud and the slime.
To Dennis Road and Colmore Road they tramped,
And sat all day in clothes that were well damped.

Some trotted north to the number four tram;
Some crossed the fields to get to Birmingham.
Bad were the means of reaching the City,
You aroused the B. T. A. Committee.

The single-man bus came to relieve us,
After much talk and after much fuss.
And we like herrings in a box did ride,
To business and school without much pride.

Down Stoney Lane to the Stratford Rd. end
No farther on the bus to depend.
In queue each morning we stood like sheep,
And heard many growls both loud and deep.

The B.T.A. up a petition drew,
Signed by a thousand and a few,
This to the Council did Dalton present,
For a through bus and all that it meant.

Now Billesley has a bus of its own,
From small things it all has grown.
With ease to the City's heart we can ride,
And smile with joy at the whole world wide.

Hurrah! for all the B. T. A. has done,
For you and for me and for everyone.
In its cap it has put a feather fine,
Long may its sun continue to shine.

(W. W., The Billesley Tenants Association Magazine, 1922)

Higher travelling costs were not the only drawbacks to living in a better house in a bright new estate. Not until 1929, 10 years after council house-building began in earnest, did the council begin to erect shops for letting on estates. Ninety were built before the policy was abandoned in 1932 under pressure from the government which believed that private enterprise should supply the need for shops. Certainly, shops were opening up on the estates, and shopping centres like Erdington, Kings Heath and Northfield were emerging as rivals to those long-established in the central and middle wards. Indeed, the decline of the Aston Road, Gooch Street, Ladypool Road, and Newtown Row shopping centres dates from the 1920s. Still, although distant they remained extremely popular with council tenants. For one thing they had more shops offering a greater variety of services. Monday morning buses from Kingstanding were known as pawn shop specials, because they carried so many women with their pawn bundles to pawnbrokers on the Aston Road. Saturdays' buses, too, were full as women went shopping to the older centres where food was cheaper and bargains could be found as butchers auctioned off their meat as night fell. The price of a tram fare could be recouped easily, but more than economics was involved in these trips. The Ladypool Road and its ilk were familiar, lively, and exciting, with their market-like flavour, bustle and characters.

60

There was everything down there (Ladypool Road). One of the finest shopping centres in Birmingham. It was a real good class shopping centre. You could get anything you wanted. All reasonable in price. Plenty of butchers' shops, hucksters' shops. You had pork butchers, offal shops, tripe shops . . . Wonderful shops.

(Mr Curtis, Chesterton Road, Sparkbrook)

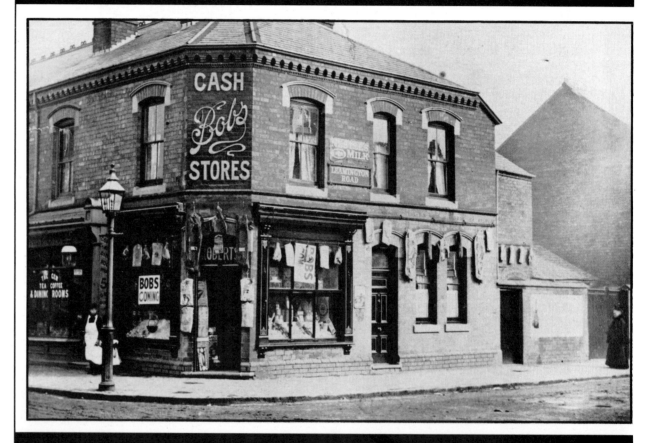

Sides of bacon hanging outside Bob's Cash Stores, corner of Ladypool Road & Leamington Road; about 1914. (Stan Jukes)

The rent on our new municipal house was 11s 4d (57p today), and the rent in Hospital Street was, I believe, about 4s 6d a week.

(Mrs Nicholson, Hospital Street and Yardley Wood)

Courtyard in Hospital Street, Summer Lane, 1920s. Like the earlier photograph of Cheapside, this yard scene is unusual in that it includes men as well as women and children. (Copec)

Higher travelling costs and dearer food were influential in dissuading some people from renting a council house. Undoubtedly, however, the greatest disadvantage of living in a newer, larger and more healthy home was its cost. The rental of a municipal dwelling was too high for poor people, even with the government subsidy and the amount allowed by the corporation under the Housing Acts. In 1933, the average weekly rent - inclusive of rates - for a parlour house was 15s 6d a week; for a non-parlour type, 11s 4d; and for smaller non-parlour houses, 8s 6d and 10s. At this level, one Birmingham councillor felt that not even a corporation employee with three children could afford to pay them except if he deprived his family of necessities. By 1941 the highest rent for municipal houses was 20s a week, and the lowest was 7s 3d, giving an average of 10s for a three-bedroomed non-parlour dwelling. By comparison, 41% of workers in the central wards were paying less than 8s a week in rent, and 71% were paying under 10s weekly. Together, the increased costs of rents, travel and shopping meant that the average working-class family in the suburbs had a cost of living 10% to 15% higher than a similar family living in one of the central wards. It is little wonder that superior housing and a better environment remained out of the reach of the poor.

Unlike Glasgow, London and Liverpool, flats were uncommon in Birmingham. Indeed, there were only three small developments of them - at Milk Street, Palmer Street and Hospital Street. It was believed that Brummies were hostile to the idea of living in flats, and they had powerful support from their Medical Officer of Health, Dr Robertson. For many years he campaigned for the building of small houses to overcome the problems of homelessness and overcrowding in the city, and in 1918 he advised strongly against the erection of flats. He was convinced that under no circumstances should they be contemplated as a substitute for back-to-backs, feeling that in time they would become even more 'unwholesome' than the dwellings they replaced. However, the realisation that the new council houses were not catering for the poor led some people to consider the building of flats. In 1923, H. Humphries, the City Engineer and Surveyor, made a report to the Public Works and Town Planning Committee which set out the predicament facing housing reformers in the city. Working-class people preferred houses, and they were a desirable form of structure; yet, if a slum clearance scheme was begun, then the bulk of dishoused people would be unable to move to the suburbs because of distance, time and increased travelling costs. Given the paucity of vacant land in the central and middle wards that was suitable and available for housing, then the only way poor people could be rehoused locally was by building flats.

. . . I respectfully submit that in dealing with the question of slum areas, it will be very difficult to carry out schemes unless . . . a certain number of flat dwellings are provided. (Mr H. Humphries, City Engineer and Surveyor, Report to the Public Works and Town Planning Committee, 1923)

These flats in Palmer Street and those in Hospital Street were the only blocks erected by private builders in Birmingham before 1914. (Bournville Village Trust)

> ... when the time is opportune for dealing with the slum question in the central areas of the City, the difficulty of obtaining sufficient land and its prohibitive cost if utilised for 'cottage building', may necessitate the Council giving very serious consideration to the erection of a number of flat dwellings ...
>
> (Public Works and Town Planning Committee, Report, 1924)

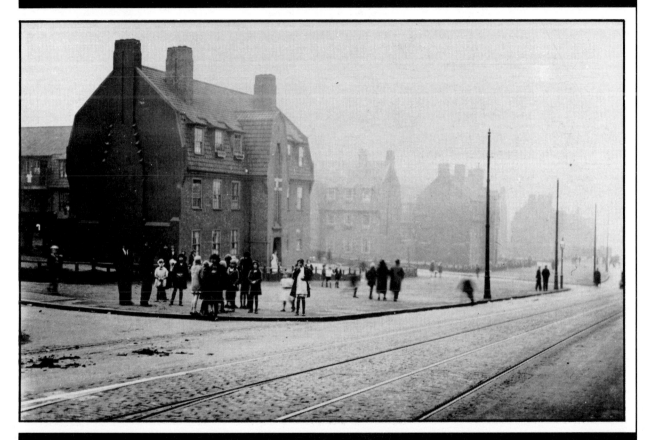

The distinctive 'Dutch-style' flats in Garrison Lane, the first flats built by Birmingham council between the wars.
(Birmingham City Council Housing Department)

In 1924, the Public Works and Town Planning Committee recognised that flats might have to be built if any slum clearance scheme was to be effective and responsive to the needs of the poor. The next year it pointed out to the council that the conditions of life in some parts of the city were no longer tolerable. Many back-to-backs were 100 years old, and were deteriorating rapidly, yet many of their tenants could not afford the rents of new council houses. Cheaper accommodation was needed desperately, and it was suggested that building costs - and so rents - could be lowered by constructing flats without baths. Accordingly, the council agreed to erect an experimental block of flats in a central district, involving the demolition of obstructive houses. The plan was abandoned because Birmingham's housing shortage was so acute that no dwellings, however undesirable, could afford to be lost. It was decided, therefore, to build on a former clay pit in Garrison Lane, near St. Andrews. In 1927, 180 flats in three storey blocks were erected. They had a distinctive 'Dutch-style' look but their tenants were not the poor for whom they had been intended. The government had insisted that baths be included in each flat, and these and other modern amenities led to a nickname of 'The Mansions' and weekly rents of from 8s 1d to 8s 10d.

Birmingham councillors were not alone in recognising that since 1919 housing policies and programmes had done little to improve the conditions of the poor. The realisation of their ineffectiveness led Arthur Greenwood, Labour's Minister of Health, to introduce in 1930 a far-reaching and momentous act which lay the foundations of modern slum clearance. For the first time a government subsidy was provided specifically for slum clearance, and it was related to the numbers of people displaced and rehoused. This was intended to prevent demolition without provision for rehousing - a practice common before 1914 and exemplified by the Corporation Street Improvement Scheme of 1875. It meant, too, that it was a subsidy on people rather than houses - a vitally important provision making it easier for councils to rehouse large, poor families because the size of the subsidy increased with that of the family rehoused. In urban areas the grant was £2 5s per person for the 40 years, plus £1 5s on the same terms if the cost of acquiring sites was unusually high and flats, not houses, had to be built. Local authorities had to make a contribution of £3 15s per house or flat for the 40 years, and the level of rents were to be at their discretion. This allowed them to adopt rebate schemes, or differential renting, provided that the rents were what tenants could be reasonably expected to pay. Finally, local authorities had to submit slum-clearance plans with the aim of solving the problem within 5 years, if possible.

My family lived up an entry in a back to back house. Rent was six shillings a week. 1 living room, 1 bedroom, 1 attic and a pantry. Gas mantle light. No running water. Coal fire. Black grate. My mother polished it with black lead till it shone.

(Mr G.W Stevens, Unett Street)

Children playing tipcat in Studley Street, Sparkbrook, mid 1930s. Lenny Preston is in the foreground. (Lily Need)

The main object should now be to build cheaper houses for the poorer people who so far have not had the chance of a house. There is a genuine desire in the City Council to fulfil this obligation, and also at the same time to provide better houses for those compelled to live in the slums. (Councillor Alderson, 1932, in, Social Questions, 1934)

3-storey back-to-backs in Florence Street, with a large factory in the background and what might be the rent man in the bowler hat; 1935. (Sylvia Leigh)

Higher rents, a dearer standard of living, and costly travel, all had made new council houses unattractive to poorer people. More than that, in common with other authorities, Birmingham council had not intended them for the poor. It had adopted the principle of only letting houses to those who could afford the rent, in effect choosing its tenants according to the same criteria as private landlords. Under the scale used in 1926, a man with a wife and three children was accepted as a 'good tenant' of a three bedroom, non-parlour house only if he earned 70s a week or more; and 80s a week was considered the minimum wage necessary for a 'good tenant' of a three-bedroom parlour home. This was at a time when a wage of 50s a week was regarded as 'good' by many working-class people. Greenwood's Act, then, at last held out the prospect of the provision of decent houses at a rental low enough for poor families. This was recognised in Birmingham, and once again a Conservative led council adopted enthusiastically an important piece of social legislation passed by a Labour Government. It informed the Ministry of Health that it intended to build 30,000 houses over the next five years - 23,000 of them under Wheatley's Act, and 7,000 as part of a plan of slum clearance.

By 1930 urgent attention was needed to slum clearance and the housing problems of the poor. Although 30,000 corporation dwellings had been built since 1919, this large figure did not even meet the requirements of the city, for by 30 June 1930 there were 31,732 applicants still waiting to be given a municipal house. Consequently, overcrowding had increased with the proportion of houses occupied by two or more families rising from 19% in 1914 to 34% in 1925. The council's ambitious housing programme in response to Greenwood's Act was essential, but it was faced by severe difficulties. Foremost was the growing shortage of land for development - a problem most pressing in the central wards where new housing was needed desperately. The building of the planned minimum of 5,000 new houses annually would require 400 acres, and that was without the needs of private development and slum clearance. In its quest for viable options for its housing programme, the council sent a deputation to Germany, Czechoslovakia and Austria to inquire in to the provision of flats for working-class people. It visited Hamburg, Berlin, Prague, Vienna, Munich, Frankfurt and Cologne, and whilst its report remained in favour of self-contained houses, it accepted that in certain circumstances flats would be satisfactory.

The problem of re-housing people under the . . . 1930 Act presents many difficulties. Some of them for obvious reasons, such as the character of their occupation, limit of means, etc., are unable to leave the central areas, proximity to their place of work being of paramount importance in some instances. Consideration of these factors suggests the possibility of having to meet the needs of these people by the provision of . . . flat dwellings . . .
(Deputation to Germany etc., Report, 1930)

Karl-Marx Hof, Vienna - high-density flats built for Austrian working-class people; 1927.
(Bournville Village Trust)

Edward, Prince of Wales, opening the Ashcroft Estate, Vauxhall, built as part of a slum clearance programme; 23rd October 1934. (Birmingham Library Services)

The necessary amenities regarded as essential if flats were to be satisfactory were possible only if the 'colony' was a large one of 500 to a 1,000 dwellings. A maximum height of four storeys was preferred, whilst the blocks ought to be laid out on town planning lines - so permitting the full enjoyment of sunshine and fresh air. Finally, the deputation recommended that up to 1,000 flats should be included in the five year programme for slum housing. Not until 1932 was any progress made in the matter. Following an article in the Evening Despatch it was agreed to build 175, two storey maisonettes in Great Brook Street, Duddeston - on the site of a former cavalry barracks. All had a large living room, scullery and bathroom and either two or three bedrooms, and they were divided in to six sections - each surrounding an asphalt area for playing and drying. Until this development, a mere 355 new dwellings had been built in the central wards since 1918. With regard to housing, time had seemed to stand still. Whilst new houses with modern amenities were erected in the suburbs, the residents of increasingly dilapidated back-to-backs had to be content with Nettlefold's turn-of-the century policy of patching and improvement. The Ashcroft Estate was the first housing development in Birmingham specifically part of a substantial slum clearance programme, but it was too small to improve the lives of all but a tiny minority of the poor.

The Ashcroft Estate had not been intended as the first development of flats in Birmingham. Following the deputation's report, a recommendation was made in 1931 that a block of flats be erected on a five acre site close to the city centre. It was bounded by Angelina, Dymoke, Leopold and Vaughan Streets, and was crossed by Emily Street. A discussion about the type of dwelling to be built there was won by those favouring maisonettes, but the city's overall housing programme was threatened by a shortage of bricklayers and plasterers and this plan was abandoned. Accordingly, the Emily Street area was chosen as the site of an experimental block of concrete flats, providing an alternative to traditional brick-constructed homes. In January 1934 the council declared the site a clearance area, and it was estimated that 257 dwellings would be required to rehouse the 1,283 people displaced by the scheme. In the event, by 1939, 267 flats with balconies were built. They varied from one to three bedrooms, were erected in four-storey blocks, and refuse disposal chutes were placed opposite all staircases. Drying rooms were provided on each floor, and there were plans for playgrounds, gardens with seats, and a bowling green. Birmingham's final development of flats before 1939 was at Kingston Road, Bordesley, where the existing property was cleared, and 98, two and three bedroom maisonettes were built in 1937. They were erected in 25 blocks and each had a sun balcony.

In April 1936, on the instructions of the City Council, the Public Works Committee promoted a successful competition for the erection of about 250 flats on the (Emily Street) site . . . (Herbert Manzoni, City Engineer and Surveyor, The Production of Fifty Thousand Municipal Houses, 1939)

The clearance of the Emily Street area for the building of St Martin's Flats; about 1937. (Birmingham Library Services)

CITY OF BIRMINGHAM. VAUGHTON STREET and EMILY STREET AREA. PROPOSAL FOR DEVELOPMENT WITH 240 FLATS FOUR STOREYS HIGH

HERBERT H. HUMPHRIES M.M CE CITY ENGINEER & SURVEYOR COUNCIL HOUSE BIRMINGHAM

Architect's drawing of proposed flats for the Emily Street area. Notice how the modernity of the flats contrasts sharply with the older housing in the background.
(Birmingham Library Services)

The council's 1930 housing programme had planned for 7,000 dwellings as part of a slum clearance scheme over the next five years. Flats and maisonettes built at Emily Street, Great Brook Street and Kingston Road did not even approach that target. The council had failed to achieve its goal and to provide effectively and substantially for the housing needs of the city's poor. Its failure was not due to any insensitivity to the plight of poor people, nor to a lack of desire to help them. Rather, the council's enterprising programme had foundered on the rock of the economic crisis on to which the nation had crashed in 1931. In an atmosphere of gloom and pessimism, and with a depression sweeping the country, high-spending housing schemes were discarded. Everywhere, retrenchment and cutting back were triumphant - Birmingham included. The supporters of economy held sway over a small minority of councillors from all parties who strove to maintain an active housing policy. Consequently, the city's housing scheme was cut and its register for municipal houses slashed. Council house-building slumped, but private building boomed. Its construction rate trebled between 1930 and 1935, increasing phenomenally from one quarter of the council's output to six times it. Home homeownership was boosted by falling construction costs, low interest rates, the approval of 90% advances to purchasers instead of 70%, and a general rise in real wages for those in work. Soon, private homes were as familiar as municipal houses in the outer ring, but their appearance - welcome as it was - did little to solve Birmingham's housing problem.

As early as 1840, a Select Committee had condemned back-to-backs as unsuitable for people to live in. Nearly 100 years later, poverty still forced tens of thousands of Brummies to rent these life-destroying houses. National and local government had failed to provide an alternative of cheaply-rented but good quality accommodation. Modern homes fitted with up-to-date conveniences were erected in the suburbs, but in the central wards the twentieth century was held at bay. Without slum clearance and rebuilding, the council's only response to the problems of bad housing remained the Edwardian policy of slum patching. In 1925 a group of Birmingham citizens realised that for the foreseeable future many people would remain living in dilapidated homes. Consequently, they formed the COPEC Society - aiming to buy slum properties and put them in as good repair as possible. The policy began in 1926 when nineteen back-to-backs in Pope Street were re-roofed, re-plastered, and re-decorated; given new floors, grates, and repaired staircases; and were installed with gas and a cold water supply. COPEC's good work continued elsewhere, but together with council's action of property improvement it barely stemmed the tide of bad housing. Indeed, many houses were beyond repair. Between 1930 and 1939, 8,000 dwellings were declared unfit and most were demolished. As had happened at the turn of the century, slum clearance without re-building could only lead to overcrowding.

70

It was therefore to the Central Wards that the newly formed society turned its attention in an effort to try to make conditions tolerable for those who would have to go on living in these worn-out older houses for a long time.

(Margaret Fenter, Copec Adventure, 1960)

The tiny downstairs room of a Birmingham back-to-back; about 1930s. Notice its cleanliness, the china cabinet and the peg rug - made from rags and old clothes - covering the floor. (Bournville Village Trust)

Communal toilets, brew 'us and miskins in courtyard back of 21, Emily Street near to Angelina Street; mid 1930s. (Sylvia Leigh)

Overcrowding was a national problem, and in 1935 an act was passed aimed at its eradication. It set a standard of accommodation and required local authorities to ascertain overcrowding in their areas and to submit a report and plans for its abatement. Crucially, provision was made for redeveloping districts where there were 50 or more working-class houses. If a third of them were overcrowded or unfit for habitation, then the locality could be declared a redevelopment area subject to a redevelopment plan. Property could be reconditioned, and the act allowed for government subsidies towards the erection of flats on expensive sites which were purchased - either to relieve overcrowding or for a redevelopment scheme. The act revived municipal house-building in Birmingham, and between the end of 1935 and 1938, 7,931 corporation houses were built as opposed to 3,851 in the previous three years. The necessity of new homes was indicated by the 1936 council report into overcrowding. It estimated that if living rooms were excluded as sleeping accommodation, then 13.5% of families were overcrowded. Moreover, there remained 38,773 back-to-backs in Birmingham; 51,794 houses without separate toilets; and despite attempts to lay on water supplies to each dwelling, 13,650 still depended on a communal tap. Over, 3,500 new houses were required to deal with statutory overcrowding, and authority was given to provide for between 1,000 and 1,500 four-bedroom homes as the first step in this programme.

71

It would have been better if more dwellings had been built during the worst years of the depression, when construction costs were low and there was unemployment in the building trade. Still, the commitment to providing new homes was welcomed by many - whatever their regrets about past policy. Yet, over the intervening years a drastic shortage of houses had accumulated, resulting in too few dwellings to meet the combined needs of slum clearance, overcrowding and normal building. Even with a renewed commitment to municipal house-building, the Estates Department indicated that only 2,200 dwellings would be completed in 1936, because of a shortage of bricklayers and plasterers. Concerned over the housing shortage, the council instructed the Estates and Public Health Committees to prepare a housing programme for a fixed period of years. Following this, the Public Works Committee was to make proposals for construction. In 1938 the magnitude of the undertaking faced by the city became apparent when the joint committee presented its report which was adopted by the council. Over the next six years a total of nearly 37,000 new dwellings were required to meet the city's needs. This figure was beyond the ability of the city to cope with, and it agreed that 25,000 dwellings were to be provided over the next five years, at the rate of 5,000 each year. A realistic hope was at last offered to tenants of unhealthy property, as slum clearance and overcrowding were to account for 4,000 of this annual figure.

72

Glover Street, mid 1930s.
(City of Birmingham Housing Department)

The Estates Committee in 1938 summarized the requirements for the next six years as follows: for normal needs, 10,038 houses; for slum clearance 23,400; for overcrowding, 3,524; a total of 36,962.
(J.T. Jones, History of the Corporation of Birmingham, Vol. V, 1940)

The crowded housing of Duddeston on the eve of redevelopment, Queen'sTower is being constructed in the background; 1953.
(City of Birmingham Housing Department)

Birmingham's post-war redevelopment was influenced heavily by three pre-war events: the 1935 Housing Act: the city's 1938 Housing Conference Report; and the appointment of Herbert Manzoni as City Engineer and Surveyor in 1935. His influence on the appearance of Birmingham was immense, and it owed much to his astute use of both national and local legislation. Taking advantage of the redevelopment provisions of the 1935 Act, he prepared a plan for 267 acres of Duddeston and Nechells. In December 1937 it was approved by the council and the district was declared a redevelopment area. The plan was acknowledged as unprecedented both in its scope as a rehousing scheme, and in its cost - about £6,000,000. It also placed Birmingham in the national limelight as it was by far the most extensive redevelopment project yet in England. Existing residential properties in the area were to be cleared and, unlike formerly, there was to be a clear separation between residential and industrial zones, as well as the provision of open spaces. By 1941 the Public Works Department was drawing up plans for another three redevelopment areas in the Gooch Street, Summer Lane and Ladywood districts. The scene was set for the transformation of the run-down central wards of Birmingham.

Manzoni's plan assumed that only about 70% of cleared residential properties would be replaced on any one site. Consequently, the remaining 30% of the population would have to be rehoused elsewhere in the city - but this would cause problems given the increasing shortage of building land in Birmingham. His solution to this dilemma relied on the recommendations of the 1938 Housing Conference Report which had altered radically the city's housing policy. Apart from the four experiments in providing flats at Garrison Lane, Great Brook Street, Emily Street, and Kingston Road, the council had insisted on building houses for working-class people. The housing shortage, and the rapid decline in land available for development, led the 1938 report to recommend that in future flats had to be an integral and esential part of the city's building programme. Thus, of the 25,000 dwellings to be built over the next five years, 15,000 were to be flats or maisonettes. As far as was practicable, they were to be built on internal sites, whilst the 10,000 houses of the programme were to be erected on land on the city's outskirts - already purchased for rehousing purposes. Manzoni's predecessor as City Engineer and Surveyor was Herbert Humphries and although he had accepted the necessity of building some flats to help in slum clearance he did not see them as a large part of the solution to the housing problem. Manzoni did, and in his influential position he was able to support and implement the change in the council's policy. The era of redevelopment and high rise flats was at hand, although it was to be postponed for ten years by The Second World War.

74

The 25,000 dwellings were fixed in the following proportions: Flats, 7,500; maisonettes, 7,500; houses, 10,000.

(J. T. Jones, History of the Corporation of Birmingham, Vol. V, 1940)

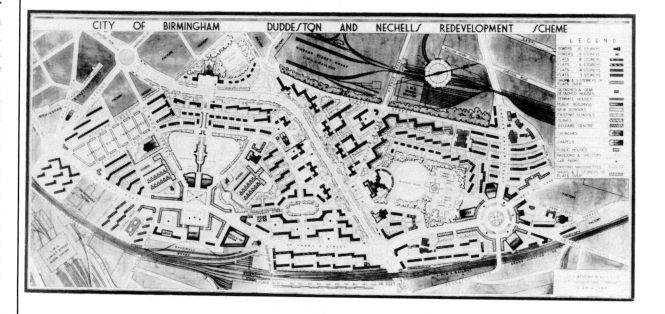

Plan indicating the separation of Nechells and Duddeston in to zones for housing, factories and open spaces.

Chapter 3: The Attack on the Slums

That was November 1940, and . . . I did, however, go to my brother's funeral, and it was a scene I can still see now. The whole of Bishop Street and Gooch Street were lined with people, crying. Almost every person there had suffered loss through the raids and that was why it was so crowded and deeply touching.

(Wyn Heywood, Belgrave Road, Balsall Heath, My Mother's Story, 1986)

Bomb damage in Bridge Street West, 30 July 1942. (Birmingham Library Services)

In August 1940 a lone German raider bombed Erdington, signalling the start of the Blitz on Birmingham. For the rest of that year, and in to 1942, the Luftwaffe pounded the city in an attempt to destroy factories as well as the determination of Brummies to defeat Hitler. Indeed, after London, Birmingham was the most-heavily bombed British city. Tragedies were numerous, especially in the poorer, central districts which bore the brunt of the Nazis' fury. One of the worst disasters of the war occurred on 25 October, 1940 when a single bomb killed nineteen people at the Carlton Picture House in Sparkbrook; and on 19 November, 1940, 350 bombers pulverised Birmingham, slaughtering about 400 people, including nearly 50 munitions workers at the B. S. A. in Small Heath. Despite the ferocity of the attacks, Brummies remained resolute against Hitler's venom; as one air-raid victim put it, 'Though our houses are down, our spirits are up'. Still, the Blitz took a terrible toll of life and health: 2,241 Brummies were killed, 3,010 were injured seriously, and 3,682 were hurt slightly. The face of the city, too, was affected badly by the raids, as familiar landmarks like the Market Hall, the Empire Music Hall and the Prince of Wales Theatre were burned out and destroyed.

During the 'phoney war' period of 1939, large numbers of Brummie children were evacuated to places less likely to be bombed. However, the delayed start to the Luftwaffe's attacks lulled people into a false sense of security, and many evacuees returned to the city just before the Blitz began. Once it started the Nazi's targeted Birmingham's poorer neighbourhoods, where houses mingled with factories turned over to the war effort. Despite the danger, there was no mass flight to the safer suburbs. Tenaciously, working-class families defied Hitler's wrath, staying in tumbledown back-to-backs which they would have been glad to leave peacefully, but not through coercion. Still, the bombings destroyed houses, and altogether 103,919 were obliterated or damaged. Of these, 4,601 were destroyed totally or were blown up so badly that demolition was necessary; 13,311 were bombed so seriously that their tenants had to be evacuated; and a further 12,126 were damaged severely but remained usable. Obviously, house-building had ceased when the war began, but the council strove to provide accommodation for those made homeless. 517 individual houses were converted in to 1,057 flatlets; 100 large dwellings became hostels for the short-term accommodation of bombed-out families; and another 801 badly-damaged houses were repaired and re-tenanted. More significantly, councillors and planners had begun to pay attention to the housing needs of the city once the war was over.

To quote "Our Mom's" actual words, she said, "Yo' ain't guin' now'ere, non' on ya' ain't, yome stoppin' 'ere with ya' fertha an' me, weem all gunna stop tergetha, that's w'at weem gunna do". This is exactly what we did . . .

Ron Smith, Quest Street, Hockley, A Paddle in Hockley Brook, n.d)

Women fitting ammunition lugs to Browning guns at the B.S.A during the Second World War. (Birmingham Library Services)

The city's growing housing stock obviously needed repairs and maintenance and College Road in Kingstanding was an early Repairs Depot.
(Birmingham City Council Housing Department)

With the outbreak of war, the Ministry of Health ordered slum clearance and construction to cease, although Birmingham continued to buy building land. Effectively, the process of redevelopment became dormant, but councillors were determined that it should not be aborted. In 1942, under the impetus of Lord Mayor Norman Tiptaft, the council established a Reconstruction Committee to co-ordinate plans to revitalise Birmingham after the war. Its grandiose ideas led to its demise in 1944, but fortunately many of its objectives were dealt with by the Public Works Committee which was committed to the task of preparing for peace time. It set up several panels to consider and advise on problems which would need urgent attention after the war, including as members representatives from commerce, industry and the professions as well as councillors. One panel concentrated on the obstacles besetting redevelopment and it instructed surveys to be drawn up of all the obsolete property in the city. Its work led to the decision to schedule for redevelopment the Bath Row, Gooch Street, Ladywood and Summer Lane areas, whilst further progress was made in 1943 when the council approved the definitive scheme for Duddeston and Nechells. Still, planners were aware acutely of the difficulty of turning ideas in to reality. Birmingham's proposals came under the 1936 Act which did not really provide for schemes of this magnitude. If massive redevelopment was to happen, then new laws were needed speedily.

During June 1943, the Ministry of Town and Country Planning set up an Advisory Panel on Redevelopment of City Centres. It sat until August 1944 and its task was to consider the best way to administer the rehabilitation of bomb-damaged towns once the war was over. Visits were made to most of the areas harmed by the Blitz, and the panel were affected deeply by the problems of cities like Coventry and Plymouth whose centres had been destroyed completely in a few nights' sustained bombing. By contrast, the attacks on Birmingham had been more drawn out and they had damaged a wider area. Consequently, its inner localities had not been 'coventried' and it would not have benefited from the panel's initial recommendations for legislation. Happily, one of its members was Herbert Manzoni, Birmingham's highly-respected city engineer. He persuaded his fellow representatives that the problems of redeveloping obsolete districts were similar to those of rehabilitating war-damaged areas, indeed probably they were more extensive. Accordingly, the Ministry accepted the panel's recommendations, passing the Town Planning Act of 1944 - also known as the Blitz and Blight Act. It gave local authorities sweeping powers of acquisition for blitzed and obsolete areas, and it included provisions for financial aid from the government. In Manzoni's words, 'the city was waiting just for this very act.'

78

He felt that the difficulties that London and Birmingham came up against led to the passing of the 1944 Act, which permitted redevelopment on a very large scale not possible before. (G. Roy Symmons, Journal of the Town Planning Institute, 1955.)

Alma Terrace, Highgate, mid 1940s. Notice the graffiti on the wall welcoming home a local man from The Second World War.
(Birmingham City Council Housing Department)

The council's programme, therefore, aims at providing 30,000 permanent high standard houses in the shortest possible time, the first year's programme aiming at 5,000 . . .
(Memorandum on Housing in Birmingham During the Post-War Period, 1944)

3 and 2-storey back-to-backs in Coleman Street, 1944. Notice the empty bottles of 'stera', sterilised milk - still popular with Brummies. (Birmingham Library Services)

Alongside its plans for redevelopment, the council paid serious attention to the city's housing problem. This was a matter of urgency given the lack of construction since 1939 and the influx of war workers to Birmingham, whilst it was to be exacerbated after 1945 by a rise in the city's birth rate. In 1944, the Public Works Committee announced its first hesitant yet ambitious proposals for a post-war housing policy. 10,000 dwellings would be required to meet the housing deficiency which existed in 1939; a further 10,000 were needed to replace homes destroyed or made uninhabitable by the bombing; 50,000 houses would have to be provided as part of a slum clearance programme; and 30,000 dwellings had to be built before December 1953 to cater for fifteen years' normal housing demands from December 1938. It was hoped that private builders would erect two-thirds of this latter figure, allowing the council to concentrate on tackling the housing deficiency and homelessness caused by the war. Consequently, it proposed to build 30,000 high standard houses in the shortest possible time, aiming at providing 5,000 of them in the first year of the programme. It was hoped that a concerted three-year attack on this part of the housing problem would then allow a huge transfer of resources to slum clearance and redevelopment. This aspect of the council's policy was acknowledged to be a much thornier difficulty which would take 20 to 30 years to complete.

Birmingham's proposals for post-war reconstruction were far-sighted and adventurous, and the city approached the coming of peace with an air of optimism. Its planning proceeded at three levels: the global, intermediate and micro. Global policy dealt with the overall, city-wide strategy for the housing programme, redevelopment and slum clearance, whilst at an intermediate layer plans were drawn up for the shape and nature of specific areas. Significantly, the design of future council estates was affected by criticisms of those built between the wars. Rightly, these had been praised for an environment superior to that of the drab central wards, but their residents had condemned their layouts as hindering neighbourliness and stifling the emergence of small, localised communities. Therefore it was decided to adopt a concept of planning based on the neighbourhood unit of the New York Regional Plan, 1928. Wherever possible, new council estates were to be considered as self-contained units of about 10,000 people. These neighbourhoods would be provided with their own shops and special buildings such as schools, community halls, branch libraries and clinics, whilst the housing was to be of all types and sizes. Ideally, also they would be economic entities so that residents could find work near to their homes and thus increase the social cohesion of the districts. This arrangement was introduced first at five large estates at Sheldon, Quinton, Harborne and Washwood Heath, and then to the redevelopment areas. It was not easy to implement, but though reality often fell short of theory, it indicated a willingness to listen to tenants.

Birmingham was launched upon an uncharted sea and, like Columbus, it believed that there was a landfall to the west but it couldn't be certain.
(Herbert Manzoni, Journal of the Town Planning Institute, 1955)

Herbert Manzoni, City Engineer and Surveyor - the man thought by many to be the architect of post-war Birmingham.

Interior of a post-war council house in Duddeston, late 1950s.
(Birmingham Library Services)

The intermediate planning level was complemented by a micro strategy which attended to the design of houses, and here again the influence of working-class people was felt. One of the city's war-time advisory committees focused on possible designs for new council houses and on the domestic equipment that they would need. It was recognised that those who knew most about this subject were the people who lived in corporation dwellings and so six Brummie housewives, all council tenants, were appointed to the committee. Its inquiries were supplemented by research which involved the construction of two model kitchens. The result of these detailed investigations was unequivocal. Post-war houses had to be roomier than those built in the inter-war years, and they had to be provided with better facilities. A standard house would remain three bedroomed, but its total area would increase from 760 square feet to 870. It would have a through hall and large living room downstairs; a bathroom and separate water closet upstairs; and at the back, a small wash-house, water closet and covered space for the dustbin. The most significant improvements were associated with the kitchen. This would be provided with built-in cupboards, a drying room, a hatch connecting it to the living room, two draining boards, a fitted table, a large cupboard for kitchen utensils, larder, coalhouse and delivery hatch.

In 1941, When We Build Again had identified reconstruction as the most important national initiative after the war effort. People seemed animated by a desire to avoid the mistakes and pitfalls which had plagued reformers after 1919. No matter how appealing, a slogan such as Homes Fit for Heroes could not build houses nor create a better world. As the Bournville Village Trust investigation indicated, if there was to be progress then central direction and inspiration were essential. No longer could Birmingham stand alone, interpreting national legislation in its own adventurous and semi-independent way for the benefit of its citizens. It could still be forward thinking, as indicated by its redevelopment schemes or its adoption of the neighbourhood unit strategy, also referred to in Abercrombie's Greater London Plan, 1944. But schemes and strategies could be implemented and made effective only with the deep involvement of central government. Thus, Birmingham's thoughtful inquiries in to the design of post-war houses were overshadowed by the contemporary Dudley Report (1944). This, too, recognised that the living space in inter-war council houses was cramped, and it acknowledged also the importance of kitchens and the need to improve facilities within new dwellings. But Birmingham's innovative research and recommendations never received the national acknowledgement they deserved precisely because they reflected national trends. Now, Birmingham was tied clearly to national policy.

Birmingham's reconstruction plans were more ambitious and advanced than those of other cities, especially in respect of slum clearance and roads. But when the war ended Birmingham's future was linked much more closely than before with that of the whole country. (Anthony Sutcliffe & Roger Smith, History of Birmingham, vol. III, 1974)

Courtyards, hidden from the street, are open to view in this aerial shot from the roof of Lucas, Great King Street, 1948. (Bournville Village Trust)

Aerial view of Duddeston and Nechells during redevelopment, dominated by the district's gas works and railway lines; mid 1950s.
(Birmingham City Council Housing Department)

With the arrival of peace in 1945, Birmingham seemed well prepared to tackle its housing problem once and for all. In most respects it was in a more advantageous position than other local authorities. It had a coherent housing programme, considered housing strategies and five defined redevelopment areas. These covered nearly 1,400 acres, of which almost 1,000 were obsolete property. All had been surveyed; draft zoning and tentative layouts had been made; the city council had given its approval of the schemes; and in February 1946 it made the Compulsory Purchase Order necessary to allow it to take over property in the areas. Thus, Birmingham was committed to the purchase of about 30,000 sub-standard dwellings, their clearance and the building of new towns on their site. Moreover, it was determined to remedy the housing deficiency by a swift building campaign so that full attention could be given to redevelopment. In this wish it was frustrated, although the newly-elected Labour government wanted to help and had set a national target of building 240,000 houses per year. In 1946 it passed a Housing Act which provided a Treasury subsidy of £16 10s per new house for 60 years, so long as the local authority gave a grant of £5 10s. However, as after 1919, aspirations were confounded by pitiless economic reality. The goodwill of the government was negated by insufficient resources stretched to breaking point by the competing claims of industrial reconstruction, nationalisation and the welfare state programmes.

Not until the summer of 1945 did the government find it able to authorise a start to building, and even then Birmingham's housing programme was threatened by severe shortages of labour and materials. The council had recognised this likelihood in 1944, anticipating that it would have to adopt unusual construction methods if it were to achieve its target of erecting 5,000 houses in the first year after the war. The desperate scarcity of skilled labour and of traditional building materials such as brick could be overcome only if houses were built non-traditionally. Birmingham was well-prepared for this eventuality. Apart from Coventry it was the only council to have experimented with building types during the war, erecting two trial steel-framed houses at Alum Rock. Their interiors were permanent and included a considerable measure of prefabrication, whilst their exteriors were clothed with temporary materials of a good quality which could be replaced later by brickwork and tile without moving out the tenants. However, by mid 1945 support had swung away from them, although 500 were put up in Sheldon in 1949 after an offer from the British Iron and Steel Corporation. Two other experimental houses were constructed. This time it was with the concrete system developed by the local firm Bryant's, but they proved too costly to be of use to the council.

In an effort to find a means to overcome this difficulty, the City Council have erected a pair of houses, the accommodation and amenities of which are a considerable improvement on pre-war Council dwellings, but which they anticipate can be erected much more quickly . . . and will involve less skilled tradesmen's labour. (Memorandum on Housing in Birmingham During the Post-War Period, 1944)

System-built council houses at Tile Cross, 1952. (Birmingham Library Services)

It has been agreed as a temporary measure that the city should take several thousand Portal dwellings to last for about ten years. Temporary buildings have a bad habit of becoming permanent.

(Alderman Tiptaft, I Saw A City, 1945)

Prefabs at The Square, Weoley Castle, 1950s. (Bournville Village Trust)

Churchill's war-time government, too, had recognised the need of erecting non-traditional houses. In 1944 it announced plans to mass produce prefabricated dwellings which could be assembled on site by unskilled labour. At first, Birmingham council was opposed to accepting any prefabs as it believed them to be an inferior form of accommodation. However, by the end of 1944 the dearth of normal building resources made this position untenable. Reluctantly, the council agreed to take 2,500 prefabs as soon as they were available, and to erect them on council-owned sites; whilst another 2,000 were to be put up on private plots. Further, wherever possible, they were to be placed on the street frontages of parks or open spaces but not on sites identified for permanent houses. These provisos, as well as a shortage of materials, meant that in 1945 only 325 temporary houses were finished, although the following year matters improved with the completion of another 1,475. Altogether 4,625 prefabs were put up, including 552 made in America and obtained under lease-lend. As predicted by Manzoni and Alderman Tiptaft, many of these temporary buildings became permanent. Some were removed in 1955-56 at the end of their intended ten year life, but 1,800 of them remained in 1972, and seventeen are tenanted still in Wake Green Road, Moseley. Indeed, though factory made, they boasted two bedrooms, fitted kitchen, toilet and bathroom. Certainly, these facilities were better than homelessness.

By 1946 prefabs were becoming familiar features in Birmingham, but the rate of construction of permanent houses was most unsatisfactory. A meagre six had been finished in 1945, with a scanty 413 the following year, and a slightly better figure of 826 in 1947. The total inadequacy of this number was emphasised when it was revealed that in the same year there were over 50,000 applicants on the city's housing register. Homelessness in Birmingham and elsewhere appeared to be an unmanageable problem. True, the major blame was a national scarcity of building materials and labour, but the council must have regretted its hasty decision not to proceed with erecting steel-framed dwellings. The dream of post-war reconstruction had become a nightmare which daily was worsening. By June 1948 the waiting list for homes had swollen to nearly 65,000 names, and the council tried desperately to stem its further increase. Exchanges and relets were increased, house-building was rationalised, and in 1949 changes were made to the points system. This had been established in 1945 to ensure a fair allocation of dwellings to applicants on the housing register, but the city's crisis of homelessness led to the introduction of a five-year residential qualification and an emphasis on housing special cases. These strategies reduced the waiting list to 50,000 names, but the building rate remained low and without a drastic increase there seemed little prospect of a further fall in homelessness.

Birmingham's housing queue is still growing at the rate of 350 a week. On 9 August there were 58,384 names on the register . . . On some days 1,000 people wanting homes plead their case at the Estates Department. Its postbag averages 500 letters a day. (Birmingham Evening Despatch, 1947)

Bleak bedroom of a back-to-back, 1950s. The lack of furniture, the unguarded stairs and the dreadful condition of the structure itself indicate the severe problems posed by poverty to many Brummies. (Bournville Village Trust)

Clara Bartholomew with neighbour's children in Barr Street, Hockley, about 1940s. (Mrs Beryl Brooks)

Nationally, building rates fell short of the Labour government's target of 240,000 houses a year; but Birmingham's progress was worse than most local authorities. During the year ending March 1949 it erected just 1.39 municipal dwellings per thousand people, compared to a national average of 3.72. Indeed, for the year ending June 1949 its production of new permanent dwellings was less than half that achieved by other large cities in England and Wales. This situation was intolerable, and after the local elections of 1949 the council set up a Standing Joint Housing Committee to investigate the city's tardy building rate. It was a cross-party group comprised of councillors from various committees concerned with housing. Since 1945 this issue had dominated local politics in Birmingham. Certainly there were differences between the Conservatives - who advocated a greater reliance on private enterprise to solve the housing problem - and Labour - who opposed the erection of experimental houses. Still, Birmingham politics was not confrontationist, indeed the Conservatives had claimed to be the most 'Socialist' of Conservative-controlled municipalities before 1939. Both parties were determined to eradicate the slums, to build as many municipal houses as possible, and to create a better environment for Brummies. Despite their political disagreements, there was a fundamental and much-needed consensus over housing policy. This boded well for an improvement in the city's building rate.

The joint Housing Conference blamed Birmingham's inferior rate of construction on the city's acute labour shortage and its wastage of the building workers available. To counter these worries it proposed that more non-traditional houses should be built. The Public Works Committee accepted this, planning to include 2,000 of them in its 1950 building programme. Moreover, it decided to abandon local construction firms which had fallen behind with their municipal contracts. Instead it would invite to Birmingham several large building concerns which were capable of erecting non-traditional dwellings on a large scale. At the same time, the council argued that the Ministry of Health had to loosen its tight control cover local-authority building so that it could plan ahead and erect more houses. This it did. These beneficial changes in local and central government policy meant that the city's building rate increased from 1,227 dwellings in 1949 to a peak of 4,744 by 1952, by when the housing register had fallen to 43,000 applicants. Vitally, both Conservative and Labour representatives had supported most of the recommendations made by the Joint Housing Committee. This harmony was crucial for the future well-being of the city. It meant that housing policy in Birmingham would remain consistent whatever political party was in control, allowing Brummies to benefit from long-term planning.

After the war, a problem, additional to that which faced most of the big cities, was that in Birmingham the shortage of skilled trades in the building industry was particularly acute owing to the attraction of factory work. At first progress was slow, but then the non-traditional, or new tradition, builders were invited to . . . the city . . .

(A. G. Sheppard Fidler, City Architect, The Builder, 1957)

Living room in council house, late 1950s, showing how even modern accommodation could be cramped if the family was large.
(Birmingham City Council Housing Department)

I remember the attic which was lit by a candle or paraffin lamp, and the bathroom and living room were lit by a mantle gas jet . . . I had to pass houses which were bombed in the war. Mom had to get up early to get the copper going with old peelings and slack we riddled out of the coal. We had an old brown crock sink, a tin bath on the cellar head for our Friday night bath.

(Mrs Cartmell, New Spring Street, Brookfields)

Gas mantle hanging from the downstairs-room ceiling of a decaying back-to-back in Gee Street; yet notice the determined efforts of the tenants to improve their home and to keep it respectable. (Copec)

In 1947 the Minister of Health confirmed Birmingham's Compulsory Purchase Order on its redevelopment areas. The scene was set for slum clearance and rehousing on a scale never before witnessed in the city, and there was little doubt that it was needed desperately. Soon after the war the council had ordered a comprehensive housing survey of Birmingham, and its results made depressing reading. Since 1936 demolitions and bombing had reduced the number of back-to-backs by nearly 10,000, but still over 29,000 were left - almost 60% of them in the redevelopment areas. There lingered around 6,500 dwellings without a separate water supply, and again 60% were in one of Birmingham's five blighted districts. 35,000 houses still had shared toilets, 81,500 had no bath, and appallingly, there remained 417 dwellings with no gas or electricity. These statistics could give only a vague impression of the distressing conditions under which tens of thousands of Brummies lived. Valiantly they defied tremendous odds, striving to lead decent lives in the most inhospitable environment. After such shocking revelations, Manzoni hoped that the council would transfer its resources to slum clearance. But it was preoccupied with the grave problem of a burgeoning housing register, and redevelopment was put on hold.

The 1947 Housing Survey Report led the Estates Committee to allocate one-quarter of all new dwellings to slum clearance. However, the current rate of building in the city was too low to allow a start to this operation and the council had to accept that large numbers of people would have to live in unacceptable accommodation for some years to come. In these circumstances it was imperative that their environment should be improved as much as possible, without too great an expenditure on houses with a low life expectancy. Therefore, the council embarked on a short-term policy of reconditioning slum property. 'Soling and heeling', as it was now called, had long been established as a central feature of Birmingham's housing programme. The Corporation Street Improvement Scheme (1875) had been the city's first involvement in redevelopment, and although it did not rehouse those made homeless under its operations it did improve 1,000 dwellings. Under the prodding of Councillor Nettlefold, reconditioning of this kind became the key element of the city's assault on the housing problem before 1914. Moreover, in the absence of redevelopment in the inter-war years, it remained a crucial strategy within the central wards, alongside the demolition of insanitary property. Slum patching it may have been, but to those who dwelt in dilapidated back-to-backs any improvement in the standard of their homes was welcome.

The toilet was at the top of the yard, there were two, but one never worked for years. It was shared by the top two families, the other six families shared the two toilets in the yard below. They were all wood with just a toilet bowl in the centre, the handle to flush was usually string. (Mrs Irene Foster, 3 back of 33 New Street Aston, rehoused 1969)

Alma Terrace, Highgate, before 'soling and heeling'; early 1950s.
(City of Birmingham Museums and Art Gallery)

> The pioneering work recently carried out by . . . Birmingham in the field of reconditioning slum houses helped to focus attention on this urgent social problem. The practical experience gained . . . was of great value to the Government in framing the Housing Repairs and Rents Act, 1954, and the City undoubtedly gave a lead to the country in "Operation Rescue".
>
> (J.P. Macey, Housing Manager, & A. G. Sheppard Fidler, City Architect, The Builder, 1955)

Alma Terrace, Highgate, after 'soling and heeling'; mid 1950s.
(City of Birmingham Museums and Art Gallery)

Through the 'expedited completion' procedure, the council was able to speed up compulsory purchase within the redevelopment areas. This time-saving measure allowed it to take over convenient blocks of property and replan their sites whilst compensation was worked out between their owners and the corporation. Once acquired, the buildings became the responsibility of the Central Areas Management Committee, set up in 1947 to oversee the work of maintenance pending redevelopment. Around 30,000 sub-standard houses came under its control, and it was estimated that it would take at least twenty years to clear them and redevelop their sites. Accordingly, the council ordered the Committee to launch an extensive programme of reconditioning, intending to make decayed dwellings tolerable to live in until they were demolished. The 1944 Act made no direct provision for improvement, nor were government grants available, so the financial burden of reconditioning fell fully on the city. Rightly it thought this expenditure was justified, and the Conservative's 1954 Housing Act vindicated the council's decision by giving government grants towards rehabilitation. Moreover, it ordered that if a local authority could not clear its slums within five years, then it must prepare schemes for improvement.

Within the redevelopment areas, sub-standard houses were improved according to their life expectancy. 'Short life' properties were those scheduled for demolition within five years of acquisition by the council. Apart from providing water supplies to some of them, repairs on these were limited to maintaining them to minimum standards laid down by the Public Health Acts. These urgent repairs and maintenance of a day-to-day nature included repairing roofs, main walls and defective drains, and making the houses wind and weather tight. Intermediate properties were those with a projected survival of five to ten years. These dwellings were repaired more extensively by attending to structural problems, defective roofs, gutters and chimneys. Work on both categories was carried out by about 100 small building firms, with a combined labour force of 1,000 men, at an average cost of £40 to £50 per house. By the end of September 1953 they had given first and interim state repairs to 25,000 houses. Some indication of the enormous size of Birmingham's housing problem is given by the survival in to the 1950s of this huge number of obsolete dwellings. The council was haunted by the city's unwanted heritage of back-to-backs. Even into the 1960s it was having to carry out maintenance work on this outdated and decayed type of housing.

17/57, Brighton Place, Abbey Street, Hockley . . . the date on the nameplate above the entry to the houses was "1874" . . . In the early 1960's the Council came and installed fire escape hatches in all the attics, comprising of a sheet of plaster board which was to be 'kicked through' in the event of fire and escape via the neighbour's house.
(Mr G. R. Hatton, Abbey Street, Hockley)

Court in Benacre Street, 1965. The survival of so many back-to-backs into the 1960s indicates the enormity of Birmingham's housing problem. The clean washing in the yard provides a link with similar photographs from the turn of the century.
(Birmingham Library Services)

Kitchen in Gee Street, about 1965. (Mrs McLauchlan)

The final category of sub-standard houses were those with a life expectancy of ten or more years, and into the 1960s they were used to accommodate families who were waiting to be rehoused in more modern dwellings. Along with some intermediate property, these long-term houses were reconditioned completely. The most common renovations carried out on them were stripping and covering roofs, renewing gutters and drain pipes, and rebuilding badly bulged or defective sections of walls. Additionally, there was complete internal repair and decorations, external painting, and the repairing of outside water closets and wash-houses. To complement the work of renovation and to complete the process of reconditioning, the council also improved the properties. This task included supplying each house with a separate water supply; and installing a separate and efficient outside water closet where the dwelling possessed its own back yard, and if it did not, providing an accessible water closet to the standard of not less than one for every two houses. Of the 25,000 dwellings repaired by the council up to March 1953, 6,480 had been renovated completely at an average cost of £195 per dwelling.

Admittedly, 'soling and heeling' was a stop-gap measure. No amount of renovation could transform a decaying back-to-back into a desirable, sanitary residence. Nevertheless, the council had no alternative. If slum clearance and rehousing had started before 1914, then Birmingham's back-to-backs would have numbered less and the remainder could have been cleared more quickly. But this was wishful thinking and the council had to deal with reality, no matter how daunting or uncomfortable a prospect that was. There were 30,000 sub-standard houses in the redevelopment areas in 1947, and by 1955, 24,000 remained standing. Financially and practically, it was impossible to remove them all and to rehouse their tenants in one fell swoop. From 1951 the formidable duty of supervising the job of repairs and renovation was the responsibility of the new Housing Management Department, now controlling all municipally-owned house property. Moreover, the 1954 Act meant that it would have to deal with another 25,000 obsolete dwellings situated outside the redevelopment areas. Rehousing difficulties meant that it was inevitable that these would have to be kept in use for longer than was desirable, and so standards of reconditioning would have to be highered.

Courtyard in Unett Street, about 1965.
(Birmingham Library Services)

My husband and I lived in an old back house at 1/351 Bridge Street West, Hockley from 1950 . . . The living room had a red quarry tiled floor which attracted great big slugs and there were silver fish round the fire grate. The built in cupboard that served as a larder had mice. The scullery, also with its quarry tiled floor had great big heaving black-beetles and the bed-rooms had bed-bugs. All these infestations were put right by fumigating the property and regularly puffing with D. D. T.
(Mrs Woodfield, Bridge Street West, Hockley)

The work is not glamorous, neither is it financially attractive, but there is no doubt that ameliorating measures of this kind ought to be carried out wherever families are compelled, through no fault of their own, to continue to live for some years in houses which are basically unfit for habitation.

(J. P. Macey, Housing Manager, & A.G. Sheppard Fidler, City Architect, The Builder, 1955)

'Soling and heeling' at 62-74, Cato Street, 1958. Notice the new bricks in front of the houses and the new chimney stacks contrasting with the older one in the background.
(Birmingham City Council Housing Department)

Soling and heeling was an interim measure. It was necessary until the building of sufficient new houses allowed the demolition of sub-standard dwellings, but attempts were made to find alternative policies. The conversion of back-to-backs appeared to be one, and in a pilot scheme eight were changed in to four self-contained 'through' houses. At a cost of £570 each the operation was expensive, but it was undertaken to provide some larger dwellings which were needed desperately for rehousing purposes. Most families living in back-to-backs needed to be moved into homes with three bedrooms, yet there was a general shortage of bigger houses which were acceptable to them. Furthermore, many residents preferred to stay in the central districts and did not want to be moved to a much more expensive post-war home in a distant part of Birmingham. Conversion was an imaginative and thoughtful action on the part of the city, but unfavourable circumstances ensured it could be only an insignificant part of its overall housing strategy for three reasons. Firstly, because it was difficult; back-to-backs were badly built and any considerable alteration in their existing walls could endanger the stability of the whole structure. Secondly, the cost was prohibitive; and lastly, conversion was impractical as it reaccommodated just four families whilst removing eight.

The council's avowed aim was to clear and rebuild its five redevelopment areas. But the city's low building rate in the late 1940s ensured that a slow start would be made to demolition. Not until the summer of 1948 were any sub-standard houses knocked down, and by March 1949 merely 270 had been removed. Despite this disappointing progress, the overall strategy of redevelopment advanced. Its principal aims were twofold. Firstly, to separate residential and industrial property into different zones. Secondly, to reduce abnormally high population densities of 150 or more people to the acre. This would 'free up' land, thus allowing more open spaces, and enabling improved road patterns, shops, services, schools and general amenities. However, the process of redevelopment itself was long-winded precisely because its objectives were so radical. It fell into seven distinct stages: design of a general layout; preparation of a programme; detailed survey; detailed layout designs; rehousing the population and reaccommodating industry and commerce; site clearance; and last of all, construction. At a cost of £17 per house, demolition was cheap, but it was one of the last stages in the operation of redevelopment and it could not begin until the city's building rate improved. This it did in the early 1950s, enabling slum clearance and rehousing to begin in earnest.

The ultimate object of acquiring the large area of the city was to demolish the old buildings and re-plan the whole area and redevelop with new buildings of a modern standard. This work is proceeding at the same time as the work of maintenance and improvement and the two programmes have necessarily to be carefully integrated. (Mr T. H. Parkinson, Deputy Town Clerk, The Municipal Journal, 1953)

Coronation Day Party in Milton Street, Summer Lane, 1953. (Elsie & George Perry)

We were married . . . in 1946. We had to stay with Mom for 2yrs and then we moved to 55 Bell Barn Road off Bristol Street . . . as we were lucky enough to get a house, because the houses were being knocked down for the building of the Flats. When we were told we were being put in a newly built house in Sheldon we were amazed and delighted because to have a garden and bathroom and all the other things we had done without for years, it was like a dream come true.

(Mrs Smith, Bell Barn Road, Sheldon)

Mrs Eileen Bickers with daughters Patricia, Wendy and Valerie in front of their council house, Garretts Green Lane, Sheldon, 1952.
(Mrs Adderley, formerly Wendy Bickers)

From 1951, under the responsibility of the newly-formed House Building Committee, estates like Kitts Green, Sheldon, Shard End, Tile Cross and Lea Hall developed into huge residential areas. Indeed, between that date and 1972 the Corporation erected nearly 83,000 houses. This was a staggering achievement by any standards, equivalent to rehousing a quarter of Birmingham's population. Nevertheless, during the 1950s the city's progress reflected national improvements in the building of council houses. That decade witnessed an easing up of the harsh economic conditions which had bedevilled the Labour administration during the 1940s. Fortunately, its successor, Macmillan's Conservative government, took the opportunity offered to it by prosperity and in the Housing Act, 1952, it increased subsidies for building. In the later 1950s its support shifted towards the private sector, but its earlier policy reaped rewards. There is little doubt that new council houses were appreciated by the homeless and those who had lived in decrepit property. Standards of house design had dropped a little from those set down by the Dudley Report but they remained far superior to back-to-backs and better than inter-war dwellings.

NEW ESTATE ON THE OUTSKIRTS OF BIRMINGHAM

When first we moved from Aston slums to Sheldon
The road unmade was like a country lane,
With jutting rocks and furrows of red mud
Gardens unfenced behind the new brick houses
Stretched, one vast field, a children's paradise
Of neck-high docks and thistles, bricks and planks,
Trees, tunnels, ground-nuts, brambles, dandelions.
We played and hid in half-constructed houses,
Dug dens in the soft clay, made friends,
For every family had three or four children;
No school was ready yet; all day we played
Black cinders lined the paths instead of paving slabs;
Our mothers scolded when we tramped them inside.
And for the first few weeks we had to cook
Camp-style, with saucepans balanced on the fire
Which blazed in the back-grate; our Dad
Luckily was a carpenter, so we had
Firewood, tables and a bench, which he
Rigged up for us. One of them is still there,
Painted blue, in Mom's kitchen,
While outside, where once the field was,
Privet hedges and high boards divided
the gardens neat with lawns and cabbage rows.
The concrete shopping centre in Pool Way
Which now seems such a monstrosity.
The grey rectangular blocks of flats beside,
We greeted once as signs of such modernity,
Thinking that Sheldon was being metropolised.

(Brenda Batts, Aston, Sheldon and Balsall Heath)

Tile Cross and Chelmsley Wood, late 1960s.
(Birmingham City Council Housing Department)

> For all members their new homes were something they had only been able to dream about a short time before. Some of them lived on caravan sites, these being very primitive at the time. Some were in rooms like us, some with parents with one or two children . . . All this was done in addition to working 44 hours per week in the factory, plus all the travelling to and fro.
>
> (Harry Smith, Northfield)

Austin Self-Build Scheme, Northfield, 1955. (Harry Smith)

The surge forward in municipal house-building during the early 1950s was matched by an upswing in the construction of homes for sale. By erecting around 20,000 houses between 1945 and 1966, private builders and housing associations provided 38 dwellings for every 100 corporation houses built. Most private developments were on small sites on the edges of Birmingham, although a lot of new building took place between 1961 and 1967 on the Calthorpe Estate in the middle ring. Elsewhere, the Bournville Village Trust built many homes for purchase, whilst continuing to erect houses for rent, in particular as part of the Shenley Neighbourhood Scheme. This joint development with the council began in the mid-1950s, and its 580 dwellings and community facilities constituted the largest single scheme embarked on by the trust since its inception. It also leased building land to an exciting self-build project started by Harry Smith at the Austin. As house-building was still rationed by central government, its 32 members had to be given building permits from the council's allocation. Forsaking any social life, the car workers devoted themselves to the scheme, becoming roofers, brickies and carpenters, and by November 1955 the last house was completed. Yet, however beneficial, neither projects like this nor private building could solve the slum problem.

By the early 1950s, Birmingham was building sufficient new houses to allow redevelopment to begin. At first sight it seemed a simple matter to knock down a slum district and rehouse its inhabitants in newly-built council houses in the suburbs. But the matter was more complicated than that just because rehousing involved people, and people have feelings. Sometimes a family was unable to leave the central wards because that was where its members found work. More usually, people were reluctant to move to the city's outer areas because they were unable or unwilling to pay the rent of a post-war council house. That of a municipally-owned back-to-back averaged 6s 3d a week (9s 3d gross), and it could be as little as five shillings weekly. By contrast, the rent of a post-war corporation dwelling was anything from a prohibitive 30s a week upwards, according to size. Even if they could afford it, such a massive increase in rent meant that families from the redevelopment areas had to rearrange their financial life. For this reason the council introduced a temporary rent rebate scheme to help them over early money difficulties. Still, it was forbidding for a family to make a direct move from a condemned house to a modern property. Instead many made an intermediary move in to a pre-war council house vacated by a family who could afford a post-war one.

The removal men moving Nellie Weir from Guildford Street, Lozells in 1968.
(Terry Weir)

The timing of the execution of the first stages of the programme has been based on the expected rate at which the housing manager can rehouse tenants from the redevelopment areas in other municipally owned houses. This is not always as simple as it appears; it is not always merely a question of offering alternative accommodation.
(The Municipal Journal 1953)

Birthday party for Gail Martin in front of 2 back of 15, Whitehouse Street, Aston - the house of her aunt, Lily Perry. Winnie and Bertie Martin are the adults at the party, the child with the glasses is Carol Gibbs from next door, and Granny Coverson is looking on across the fence. (Winnie Martin)

Despite a general desire for better houses and an improved environment, finance was not the only reason for people rejecting moves away from the city's central neighbourhoods. Familiarity was at least as strong a motive, and possibly it was more powerful. Definitely, it was more difficult for the council to cope with. Officials could recognise and assist with economic disincentives to move. What they found impossible to deal with was families who wanted modern houses but did not want to move. In order to survive against the depredations of poverty, poorer Brummies had established themselves in highly-localised, closely-knit communities. Families like the Careys, Masons, and Hickmans of Studley Street, Sparkbrook could trace their residence in one street, let alone a neighbourhood, back in to the 1870s and before. It was a similar story elsewhere in old Birmingham where long-established families inter-married with one another, creating close bonds of kinship within a street. Rarely did a member of a local clan move or wish to. They knew no other life, but more than that, they were aware of the support they would receive from their near and distant relatives if they were in trouble. Living so closely together in urban villages could be claustrophobic, but it was also safe and familiar. Understandably, many were loath to leave its security.

101

BAD TIMES AND WORSE TIMES

It's true that times were very hard
When we lived in a slum with a blue brick
yard.
But the money that we had was spent
On the essentials of life - food, clothes, rent.

Folks pulled together and you never saw
frowns
when we went to school in hand-me-downs

When work had gone and we kids were thin
we had our neighbours popping in
with a bit of this and a little that.
Hardly enough to feed a cat.

But we survived and now today
I smile to myself when people say
they can't manage and times are tough.
Two cars and a telly are not enough.

But they have never lived on bread and lard
and played 'I ackey' in a blue brick yard.

(Arthur Wilkes, Sutherland Street, Aston, & Hall Green)

102

*Neighbours chatting outside their homes in Vaughton Street - an area later cleared
and redeveloped with flats and maisonettes; Picture Post, 1954.
(The Hulton-Deutsch collection)*

Children in Gee Street, about 1965. (Mrs McLauchlan)

BRUMMAGEM COURTYARD

Born in a Brummagem courtyard
which was built in Victoria's days.
The back to back old houses in crumbling old bricks,
which seldom saw the sun's rays.

Us kids played summat like football,
scored goals with some brick end or tins.
Tore holes in our hand-me-down clothing
had bruises, cuts on our shins.

And the wenches pulled dolls round our courtyard,
and they'd pat 'em, and scold 'em and nag.
And they'd treat 'em like real proper babbys,
the dolls made from sawdust and rag.

Then a man from the council decided
that all of us lived in a slum.
So they pulled down our Brummagem courtyard
and we were scattered all over Old Brum.

That's summat that people call progress,
but I'd go back today if I could,
to play marlies and tip cat, and 'op, skip an' jump,
in that courtyard in old Ladywood.

(Syd Garrett, Monument Road, Ladywood & Bartley Green)

Many people had well-founded misgivings about having to be rehoused, but few could disagree that the city's back-to-backs were beyond redemption. Paradoxically, their dense packing had fostered the closeness of their residents, but their bad construction and appallingly inadequate facilities sounded the death knell for the communities which had grown up around them. In many respects, traditional Brummie working-class life was born and died with the building and demolition of Birmingham's back-to-backs. The end was heralded in 1950 by the clearance of the redevelopment unit around Great Francis Street and Bloomsbury Street. Each of Birmingham's five redevelopment areas was too large to deal with en bloc, so they were sub-divided in to smaller sections like this one in Nechells. They formed small separate redevelopment schemes and by 1953, fourteen were planned and in some stage of redevelopment, whilst four of them had been cleared of existing property and rebuilding had begun. The first large building to be completed was Queen's Tower, at the junction of Great Lister Street and Great Francis Street. It was opened officially in 1954 by the Minister of Housing and Local Government, and was one of four twelve-storey blocks of flats.

It was up an entry and it had no sink but a tap on the wall outside. It had gas light . . . the Brewhouse was up the yard and I used to take slack and coke and potato peelings to shovel on the fire to hot the water for the washing . . . after that I had to clean the lavatory . . . I shared . . . Well by 1956 . . . we had been invaded by rats. I went into the wardrobe and Bill's suit which was his wedding suit had the complete leg eaten. That was enough. The Council rehoused us.
(Beryl Brookes, Vauxhall Street and Billesley)

Courtyard in Gee Street, about 1965. (Mrs McLauchlan)

The clearance of Birmingham's back-to-backs was essential if a healthier and more attractive environment was to be created for Brummies. But it put councillors and planners in a quandary: where were they to rehouse those made homeless by the redevelopment schemes? These areas had very high population densities and it was found in 1953 that for every new dwelling built in them 2.2 families had to be rehoused. There were two reasons for this imbalance: firstly, because of lodgers; and secondly, because the overall population density of the districts was lowered under the city's Development Plan. This had been prepared under the 1947 Town and Country Planning Act, and it divided Birmingham into an inner zone with 75-120 persons per acre, and an outer zone with a population density of 50 people to the acre. These figures meant that many of those removed from the redevelopment areas could not be rehoused within them; indeed, in 1955 it was estimated that about half would have to move away. Consequently, the council's predicament about rehousing now encompassed the whole city, but it found no solution in the suburbs. Quite simply, Birmingham was running out of land everywhere within its boundaries. Soon it would have nowhere left to build new homes.

Children playing outside flats in Nechells; early 1960s.
(Robinson thesis, Birmingham Library Services)

It has become fashionable to decry the record of the right-wing leadership of the Birmingham Labour Group in the 1950s. Few now would defend high-rise flats as ideal homes for the elderly, families with young children, and others. Planners and councillors must regret, too, their unawareness or unmindfulness of the complex, localised communities which had taken so long to grow but were destroyed so rapidly. How much better it would have been if slum clearance had been more thoughtful; if neighbourhoods had been demolished one by one, allowing their families to be rehoused within their own communities. How much better it would have been if houses had been built and not flats. Yet 'if' is a great deceiver. It appears only to those with hindsight, those who can judge precisely because they have more information than people at the time. But there is little romantic in burning bugs from the attic ceiling before bed-time; nostalgia cannot thrive on a night-time walk through an unlit courtyard to a cold and uncomfortable outside toilet. Men like Sir Frank Price and Harry Watton knew this. They wanted to build quickly a better environment for their people. Tragically, they were unaware that the price to be paid was a loss of community spirit and a decline in neighbourliness.

Nellie Weir, in 1968 reluctantly leaving her home of over forty years, 4 back of 129, Guildford Street, Lozells, Birmingham. M.P Denis Howell lived next door.
(Terry Weir)

Clearing away the stigma of 30,000 back-to-back fetid slum dwellings and other blighted and blitzed property was, and still is, one of the most fulfilling periods of my life. The fact that we had little land to house 50,000 homeless families, and over 100,000 more to be rehoused from the slums, that there were no New Towns, made our task look almost impossible. We had no other choice but to go up.
(Sir Frank Price, ex-Chairman The Public Works Committee & Labour leader of the council, Sunday Mercury, 1990)

The house building committee was aiming at designing layouts to provide in the schemes of redevelopment for multi-storey flats not exceeding six storeys in height, together with maisonettes, three-storey flats and also normal one- and two-bedroomed houses. (Alderman A. F. Bradbeer, Chairman House Building Committee, The Builder, 1954)

Millpool Hill Estate, Warstock, 1960, showing a mixed development of multi-storey flats and housing. (Birmingham Library Services)

In 1952, A. G. Sheppard Fidler was appointed City Architect of Birmingham, becoming responsible for the design and layout of all municipal estates. Along with others, he realised that Birmingham was using up its available land supplies rapidly by building at low population densities. His answer to the problem was the redevelopment of mixed estates, a strategy he had pursued enthusiastically as architect to Crawley New Town. In the future, all municipal housing schemes in Birmingham would include a mixture of multi-storey flats and low-rise dwellings such as houses and maisonettes. Accordingly, high-rise flats would be built in the suburbs as well as in the redevelopment areas. Indeed, the first erected in the city were not in Nechells but in Tile Cross in 1953. Yet doubts were expressed as to the cost-effectiveness of erecting multi-storey flats. The contractor of the Great Francis Street scheme lost £57,000, and in 1954 the Chairman of the House Building Committee reported that their expense was such as to 'frighten the most stout-hearted taxpayer and ratepayer.' However, the pressure on the city's land supplies showed no sign of abating, even though in 1952 it acquired the Kingshurst Hall Estate outside its boundaries in Warwickshire. In these circumstances it was inevitable that the city would have to adopt higher population densities for the redevelopment areas so as to keep more people within them.

The mixed development of Kingshurst provided housing for 7,000 people and its design won a Civic Trust Award in 1963. Elsewhere in the city, the need to rehouse people on an ever-decreasing stock of land meant that blocks of flats became higher. Twenty-storey flats were erected in Newtown, and the tallest of all were the 32-storey Sentinel blocks built at Lee Bank. Yet as the tower blocks stretched ever upwards so too increased the dissatisfaction and disillusion of their tenants. The euphoria of the homeless people rehoused in Queen's Tower was short-lived. In particular, they had praised the facilities within the two-bedroomed flats: the large, light kitchen with the ingenious refuse system whereby everything - even bottles - could be disposed of down the kitchen sink; the good-sized living room; airing and store cupboards; fitted wardrobes and kitchen cabinets; bathroom with a hot towel rack and separate toilet; a verandah leading to the fire escape; and, finally, a drying balcony for clothing. But soon it was realised that these welcome facilities were not everything. A community spirit could not be manufactured alongside the building of flats. It had to grow and be nourished and the flats seemed to hinder that process.

'Lovely', 'ideal' and 'couldn't want anything better' were typical comments. Points which came in for early approval were the central heating, the ingenious refuse disposal system . . . the floor tiling and the built-in cupboards. Most of them told stories of many years spent living in one or two rooms or with relatives. The flats are the first real homes of their own they have ever had . . .
(Birmingham Evening Despatch, 1954: reactions of the first tenants in Queen's Tower, Nechells)

The installation of the community heating system at Queen's Tower, Nechells, fired by rubbish from the flats' waste disposal system; about 1953.
(Birmingham City Council Housing Department)

> They were really not the good old days as far as cash was concerned, but the friendliness and help every one received was much different than today. People seemed to understand and had time for one another.
>
> (Joyce L. Boxley, Baker Street, Small Heath and Halesowen)

Corner shop at 74, Edward Street, Ladywood, late 1950s. Left to right: Eric Davis (owner), Edna Kelly (sister), Ellen Davis (mother) and Mrs Lawrence (neighbour).
(Mrs Pat Newman)

The strategy of mixed development on estates planned on the idea of neighbourhood units had seemed a positive one. However, people began to recognise the faults in a policy which sought to impose a communal feeling on residents. In the white heat of modernisation and progress it was forgotten, or overlooked, that no amount of social engineering could make people know each other. Neighbourliness had to evolve; it was a gradual process based on daily contact, local knowledge and informal meetings. Living in flats made these day-to-day occurrences more difficult. They prevented the emergence of a true neighbourhood based on neighbours who were aware of each other. Residents felt isolated in their flats, cut off from their fellow tenants by a lack of unofficial meeting places. The street and its extensions had been the pivot of working-class life in Birmingham's poorer neighbourhoods. Surrounded by children playing, women had met, worked and chatted in the brew'us and the yard. They had shopped on tic in intimate corner shops, pledged their belongings in well-known pawn shops, and like men and teenagers they had gathered in casual street-corner groups, enveloped by gangs of children. Street bookies took bets, and people drank in small, familiar pubs which belonged to their street. Neighbours laughed, danced and partied, cried, argued and fought in the street. They belonged to the street. But its significance unrealised till too late, street life fell a victim to redevelopment.

Not every rehoused person mourned the passing of their former neighbourhood. Certainly, all those moved appreciated the benefit of more rooms, modern facilities, and - most luxurious of all - their own toilet and bath, with hot as well as cold water. Many found themselves with front and back gardens and recreation grounds nearby, increasing the attractiveness of their new homes. Large numbers of them had loathed the insanitary conditions in which once they had been forced to live. On their balance sheet a vastly improved environment - especially for their children - more than made up for the loss of a close-knit community. Others viewed the parochialism of their old neighbourhoods with distaste, seeing it as stifling and inward-looking, not supportive and safe. Whatever the viewpoint of working-class people, they could do little to halt the transformation of their city. Even the names of the redevelopment areas were altered along with their housing, although Ladywood was retained because it was pleasant-sounding. Nechells had Green added to it to reflect the pleasing parkway which intersected the district; the Gooch Street neighbourhood was renamed Highgate; Summer Lane became Newtown; and the Bath Row area was changed to Lee Bank.

I had fallen in love with Northfield . . . After a weekend of weighing the pros and cons, like distances from work and school, we decided to move . . . Mom's brows shot up when I told her I was leaving Sparkbrook. "Whatever for?" she wanted to know . . . Had she ever taken a good look at Struggling Manor, I wondered? Had she really never noticed how I'd hated the very bricks, mortar and dirty rain puddles of the place?
(Lily Need, Struggling Manor, n.d., Studley Street, Sparkbrook, Northfield and Tamworth.)

Terrace of back-to-backs in Studley Street, Sparkbrook prior to demolition; mid 1960s. The spire of St Agatha's Church, Stratford Road is in the background. (Lily Need)

There is a strong case for founding one or more satellite towns to rehouse some of the worst accommodated scattered factories, together with workers from older parts of the city . . . The sites for such towns would have to be far enough out of Birmingham to assure individuality and avoid the danger of becoming mere dormitories; a satellite town is not a suburb . . .   (When We Build Again, 1941)

Overspill housing at Telford new town, late 1960s.
(Birmingham City Council Housing Department)

Despite the increased antipathy towards high-rise flats, the council had little alternative but to continue to build upwards in the 1950s. Particularly in the redevelopment areas, taller buildings increased population densities drastically, to as high as 153 persons to the acre in the Great Francis Street unit. Yet even this allowed the replacement of only 56% of the dwellings in these districts. In all, a surplus population of 49,000 would have to be rehoused elsewhere. The question was, where? During the inter-war years the city had been fortunate to be able to build on large reserves of land acquired by its extension in 1911. These were no longer available and a further expansion seemed unlikely. Even the acquisition of a green-field site like the 252-acre Kingshurst estate could do little but staunch the outward flow of families from the central wards. In these adverse circumstances the council sought a solution advocated as early as 1941 by When We Build Again. With adjoining county councils it negotiated agreements to take some of Birmingham's overspill population. Eventually, schemes were agreed with Droitwich, Tamworth, Redditch and Daventry, and Brummies were dispersed into Worcestershire, Staffordshire and Northamptonshire. But in the long-term this overspill had little effect on the city's overall housing problem.

Following the 1954 Housing Act, the council drew up schemes to deal with obsolescent property outside its five blighted districts, and in 1955 it defined a further fifteen redevelopment areas. With about 30,000 people, and covering around 1,700 acres, they encircled the city centre, filling in the gaps between the localities scheduled originally. Although stretching in to the city's Middle Ring, effectively they encompassed the Central Wards and most of Birmingham's back-to-back housing. Hockley, Lozells, Gosta Green, Winson Green, Bordesley and much of Aston, Balsall Heath, Bordesley Green and Small Heath were set to be transformed, though large-scale acquisition was not possible as in 1946. Still, by 1960 the council was managing 12,000 houses in the new zones, and by 1963, 6,000 properties had been reconditioned. Unhappily, the expansion of the redevelopment programme coincided with a drastic decline in the city's building rate, which fell below 2,500 completed dwellings in 1958 and dropped to just over 2,000 between then and 1961. This was not deliberate policy, but Birmingham's dire shortage of land meant the construction of increased numbers of multi-storey dwellings which were costlier, slower to erect and more labour intensive than house-building. Secondly, it caused the development of sites unsuitable for building because of difficulty of access, irregularity of level and shape, and poorness of load-bearing soil.

The proportion of multi-storey dwellings in the city's housing programme has been steadily rising over the past five years in order to get the maximum value out of the limited amount of land now available in the city ... Multi-storey dwellings are more expensive and they take more labour to build than two-storey houses.

(The Surveyor, 1956)

The 1st Wates Build multi-storey flats in Birmingham - built late 1960s-early 1970s, at Primrose Hill, Kings Norton. (Birmingham City Council Housing Department)

... the housing management have a waiting list of sixty-five thousand people for new houses or flats. Some have been on the list for fifteen years. Top priority has to go to those with large families.

(Picture Post, 1956)

Mr & Mrs H.J. Murray, evicted from their lodgings after 11 years - through no fault of their own - queuing at the Birmingham City Council Housing Management & Welfare Offices; Picture Post, 1956. (The Hulton-Deutsch collection)

The unavoidable fall in Birmingham's building rate ensured that once again its housing register rose sharply, peaking at over 70,000 applicants in 1958. This unrelenting advance in homelessness placed the council in a familiar predicament; who should be given priority in rehousing? The slum clearance campaign had to continue apace because it was intolerable that so many Brummies still lived in ramshackle back-to-backs; and secondly, because the scarcity of building land meant that the council's housing programme depended upon the provision of cleared, central sites. Accordingly, about 60% of new municipal dwellings were allocated to those made homeless by redevelopment, and the remainder to those with a high priority - especially to large families. Under pressure from the housing crisis the council adhered strictly to its rule of only reaccommodating people who had lived in Birmingham for five years. Critics believed that this policy discriminated against Indian and West Indian families and led to the emergence of ghettos. Certainly, hard-working black immigrants had cause to feel aggrieved at its effects, but the rule was not racial in intent. It was passed in 1949, before large-scale post-war immigration from the Commonwealth; and it was aimed at the many English, Scottish, Welsh and Irish workers who had flocked to the city recently. Given Birmingham's dire housing problem, the council felt it had to concentrate its resources not on newcomers, but on rehousing those who for years, perhaps decades, had lived in dreadful conditions.

Birmingham's low building rate continued in to the early 1960s, but from 1962 its housing situation began to improve under the guidance of Councillor Ernest Bond, Labour chairman of the House Building Committee. He made considerable changes in the administration of his department, and new strategies were adopted to ease the city's housing crisis. For example, the proportion of one-bedroomed homes was increased, allowing elderly tenants to move out from larger houses and thus making them available for families; new types of industrialised dwellings were considered; more high-density building sites were leased from the Calthorpe Estate; and a campaign by the Liberal Councillor, Wallace Lawler, led to construction schemes with various housing associations. Still, the building rate remained under 2,500 dwellings per year until 1965 when the figure rose dramatically to over 4,000. This was thanks to the development of the huge Castle Vale Estate, five miles from the centre of Birmingham. It was located close to major employers such as Fisher and Ludlow, Dunlop, Lucas and Morris Commercial and so proved popular with existing council tenants; indeed, 78% of the estate's households were 'transfers'. However, many soon became disillusioned with a lack of community and shopping facilities, as well as with life in high-rise flats.

"It was built on the old Castle Bromwich airfield and I remember arguing with the then housing minister, that educated idiot Richard Crossman. I pleaded with him to keep one of the old hangars as a community centre but he gave me a tongue-lashing for being so old-fashioned. But it was madness to build estates like that without proper community facilities.

(Sir Frank Price, formerly Labour leader of Birmingham council, Sunday Mercury, 1989, talking about the Castle Vale Estate)

Aerial view of Tile Cross in the foreground and Chelmsley Wood in the background.
(Birmingham City Council Housing Department)

Most of my constituency advice bureaux are concerned with people living in high-rise flats .... It is not the accommodation that worries them, but the total environment in which they live. Their health is suffering and they feel they have to get out. They are being isolated in high tower blocks and the sense of community spirit is broken down. (Ray Carter, Labour M.P., Birmingham Northfield, Birmingham Evening Mail, 1970)

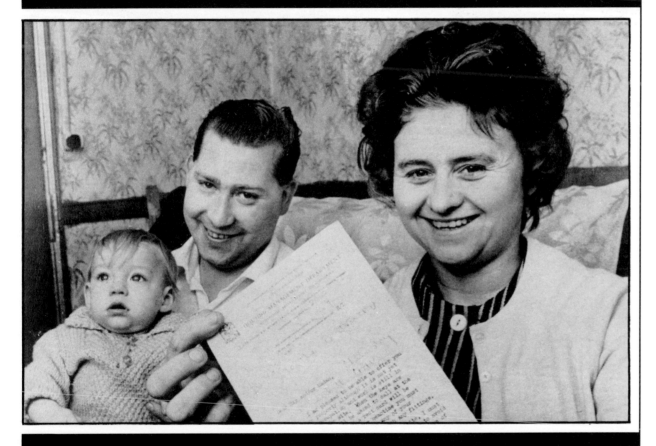

The first tenants on the Chelmsley Wood Estate - looking forward to a new home after years spent living in slum housing. (Birmingham City Council Housing Department)

High-rise flats dominated the skyline of new corporation estates, but familiarity did not bring popularity and in 1958 the city's housing manager admitted that 80% of flat dwellers disliked their homes. From 1954, in reaction to this aversion of Brummies, the council extensively built two-storey maisonettes in blocks of four stories, but as late as 1965, 77% of new council dwellings were flats. They were particularly unsuitable accommodation for families with children, yet at Castle Vale - where in the 1960s nearly a third of the estate's population was fourteen or under - 60% of the homes were flats. An antipathy to flat life was matched by a dissatisfaction with the facilities on post-war estates, mirroring the complaints made by tenants on new estates in the inter-war years. In 1951 Sheldon had one shop for every 228 residents, compared to a city average of one to 56 people. The next year the council decided that new estates would be provided with one shop for every 100 inhabitants. Though they were to be grouped in larger centres, no house would be more than a quarter of a mile from shopping and isolated general stores would be allowed where essential. Matters improved, but in 1959 the general lack of amenities at Kingshurst led the Evening Mail to describe tenants there as 'Lonely Exiles'.

From the mid 1950s, most shops on new estates were ready before the arrival of the first tenants. Unfortunately, not always were they occupied, as shopkeepers often waited for the population to increase before they opened for business. The council could not be blamed for this, nor for the lack of picture houses and other facilities provided by private enterprise. However, with local breweries it was responsible for fewer pubs in new areas, and it could be faulted for a shortage of community centres - although some people regarded central government as the real culprit, because of its close supervision of local authority developments. Certainly, the council could not be held responsible for unsatisfactory postal and telephone facilities, both of which were outside its control. Further, many complaints by tenants about life on a new estate were intangible, reflecting a sense of loss for the communities that had been destroyed with the redevelopment of the central wards. But regret at the passing of a way of life could not hide the fact that more and better houses had to be built for Brummies. In the mid 1960s thousands of people remained living in back-to-backs. They could not be rehoused until the city's building rate improved drastically. The development of Castle Vale and Bromford Bridge made this possible, and from 1966 the Conservative-controlled council continued the good work of its Labour predecessors.

As far as the provision of municipal homes is concerned Birmingham has held the blue riband for the past four years and in the past three years has built more houses than any other three comparable local authorities put together.

(Alderman A.M. Beaumont Dark, Conservative Chairman, Birmingham Housing Committee, Birmingham Evening Mail, 1970)

Modern council housing at Cambridge Drive, Marston Green; early 1970s.
(Birmingham City Council Housing Department)

The Bromford Estate, 1967, before work began on redeveloping the site of the former Birmingham Racecourse.
(Birmingham City Council Housing Department)

In 1966 the council completed the building of 4,775 dwellings; the next year the figure rose spectacularly to 9,034 and although it fell back to 7,300 in 1969, the total of 30,000 homes completed over the four year period was greeted as a 'world record'. Under the chairmanship of the Conservative Alderman Apps, the council's House Building Committee rebuilt Birmingham at a rate faster than any other city in Europe, this putting the city in the national and international spotlight. By 1967 it was rehousing 17,000 people a year and its horrendous waiting list was slashed by over half from its peak in 1958, falling to 31,506 applicants. The huge increase in the building rate would not have been possible without two factors: firstly, the widespread adoption of industrialised building methods, so that much of a high-rise flat was prefabricated and made simpler and quicker to erect; and secondly, the acquisition of a huge estate outside the city boundaries, for which the city had been pressing since the 1950s. Its pleas for more land had been rejected by the Conservative government, but in 1964 the newly-elected Labour administration agreed to its takeover of the estate at Water Orton in Meriden. Together with the development of Castle Vale and Bromford Bridge, the transformation of this rural district in to the township of Chelmsley Wood enabled a final onslaught on the obstinate remnants of back-to-back and obsolescent housing in Birmingham.

Almost 100 years after Birmingham's first improvement scheme, it appeared that the city's intractable housing problem was to be solved. By the late 1960s the last residents of back-to-backs were rehoused, and the dwellings which had characterised the city's housing stock since the Industrial Revolution were swept in to oblivion. The development of Chelmsley Wood provided the last weapon needed for the council's ultimate victory over its old adversary, an enemy which had killed, maimed and marred the lives of so many Brummies. Between 1955 and 1964, the city's low building rate had allowed the council to demolish just 16,000 dwellings. Now, freed from the constraints imposed by its land shortage, it was able to clear another 22,000 in just five years between 1965 and 1969. Only 13,000 houses were left of the 51,000 the council had scheduled as unfit soon after the war, and most of the original central redevelopment areas had been cleared. After a long war of attrition, the city had rid itself of the bitter legacy bequeathed it by unplanned and ill-considered urban growth in the Victorian age. Well-founded nostalgia for a disappeared communal way of life could not detract from the benefits of better housing. The scale of redevelopment in Birmingham was unsurpassed by any other British city, and rightly both Conservative and Labour councillors could be proud of their joint achievement. But the task of rebuilding was not complete. Much insanitary property remained, and by 1972 the building rate had slumped to less than 1,500 completed dwellings per year as once again building land ran out.

Has the steam gone out of Birmingham's housing drive? The figures, if not the facts, suggest an answer in the affirmative.

(Birmingham Evening Mail, 1972)

The development of Chelmsley Wood in 1970, enabled the council to make a determined attack on the city's slum problem.
(Birmingham City Council Housing Department)

The city's tallest high-rise flats, the 32-storey Sentinels blocks in Lea Bank, built in 1971.
(Birmingham City Council Housing Department)

As usual, the city's housing register acted as a barometer to the council's building rate. In 1971, following the construction boom, the waiting list for a new home had dropped to 20,000 applicants; by the next year, as the building rate slumped, it had expanded to 24,000, and by 1973 it had swollen to 29,000. Yet again, the council desperately sought to staunch the surge in homelessness, and as in the past its strategies were determined by the availability of building land. Since the early 1900s, Birmingham's hunger for land had determined its relationship with neighbouring authorities and had dictated its housing policy. In the inter-war years it was able to build houses because of the plentiful supplies of rural land swallowed up by the city's extension in 1911. The land scarcity of the post-war years meant that high-rise flats then became the solution to the city's housing crisis, but by the early 1970s they had ceased to be regarded as the panacea to its housing ills. They were expensive to build and to maintain - indeed from 1969, following the Ronan Point disaster, system-built flats had to be strengthened; moreover, most tenants disliked them vehemently. Consequently, the development at Chelmsley Wood signalled the end of building high-rise flats on a massive scale, and only 10-15% of the dwellings there were in this type of building. In these circumstances, an increase in the building rate could be achieved only by acquiring more land.

The council was acutely aware that it had to acquire rural land if it were to build houses for Birmingham's homeless and to reaccommodate those who lived in the 14,000 overcrowded and appalling slum dwellings which remained in 1972. After intense pressure, the government allowed it to develop four sites in North Worcestershire - Hawkesley, Frankley, Walker's Heath, and Kitwell. Though less than half the land it sought, building here and at Moneyhull allowed the council to accommodate over 20,000 people. Significantly, high-density development was achieved without erecting multi-storey flats. Frankley was different, also, from other post-war estates in that it symbolised landscape architecture. Since the late 1950s there had been a move away from the 'bulldozing' approach pursued in the central redevelopment areas. Indeed, the city's Architect's Department was admired for the layout of estates like Lyndhurst (Erdington, 1958) and Primrose Hill (1963). From 1966, under the direction of J.A Maudsley, the new City Architect, layout became increasingly important. In particular, landscape architecture was encouraged, and in 1970 the city received a Ministry of Housing award for designing the integrated community of 50,000 people at Chelmsley Wood. Frankley gave even more scope for the implementation of ideas about environmental planning.

120

"The best place we've ever lived in", said 62 year old Albert Cockbill. He and his wife, Violet, moved into their two-bedroomed house at Hawkesley last June. "It's the first garden I've ever had", said Albert, proudly showing rose bushes and vegetable patch. "We didn't have any of this in our fifteenth floor Kings Norton flat".

(Michael Pollack, Sunday Mercury, 1977)

Council housing at Hawkesley, mid 1970s.
(Birmingham City Council Housing Department)

Council housing at Frankley, Birmingham's last large-scale council-house development; mid 1970s. (Birmingham City Council Housing Department)

Several strategies were adopted to give a rural 'feel' to the developments at Frankley: natural features such as streams, trees, grassland and hedges were kept, and houses were integrated with them; roads were not made straight but were gently curved; and homes were built clustered in small cul-de-sacs. The long rows of uniform housing of the inter-war years and the high-rise flats of the post-war period gave way to more imaginative structures: short terraces of homes were built next to semi-detached houses of two, three and four bedrooms; red-brick dwellings adjoined those of orange; tile-hung homes were by those which were wood-faced; and houses with Spanish-style windows were close to those with more traditional windows. Importantly, serious attempts were made to avoid the communal problems associated with previous council estates. The lesson had been learned that neither councillors nor officials could make a community spirit emerge. What they could do was provide facilities which would help this process rather than hinder it. Thus, at Frankley itself the population of 12,000 was housed in two similar-sized units, each with primary and middle schools, shops, a tenants' hall, public houses and other community facilities; and the units were separated by a broad wedge of open space and the main shopping centre and secondary school. Unfortunately, these sensitive plans arrived as the era of council-house building closed.

As in the past, local authority action in Birmingham during the 1960s and early 1970s was symbolic of the thrust of national policy. For much of this period both Conservative and Labour governments acknowledged the need to demolish the slums and to subsidise the building of large numbers of municipal houses. In the early and mid-1960s national and local initiatives complemented each other as governments encouraged councils to build high-rise flats and to make use of industrialised building methods. By the late 1960s, Birmingham's reaction against both these strategies reflected national concern with their shortcomings. In 1967, the Labour administration ended the higher subsidy for structures above six stories, and the partial collapse of Ronan Point led to the decline in industrialised building. Two years later, as money for subsidies dwindled, it passed a Housing Act which heralded a housing strategy based on the rehabilitation of existing dwellings rather than massive schemes of clearance and redevelopment. This trend to the improvement of older stock was enhanced by the Housing Acts of 1971 and 1974, passed by a Conservative government. The decline of council-house building in Birmingham must be viewed in the light of these shifts in the policy of national governments. Consequently, at the same time as Frankley was developed, the council implemented a programme of urban renewal.

Chapter 4: The Future?

Birmingham City Council is launching a drive to publicise its huge seven-year urban renewal plan designed to give older housing areas a new lease of life. The overall objective is to improve and retain thousands of homes that can be modernised to avoid large-scale clearance and rebuilding. *(Birmingham Evening Mail, 1973)*

Housing in Balsall Heath, illustrating the decay of tunnel-back housing by the late 1960s and indicating the on-going nature of the battle to eradicate slum housing in Birmingham. (Birmingham Library Services)

Rear of Lawrence Street council houses before clearance; built 1891, demolished 1971.
(Bournville Village Trust)

By 1977, Birmingham's housing register had been reduced to 11,500 applicants as families moved in to new homes at Frankley and in the overspill towns of Daventry, Redditch, Tamworth and Droitwich. The council intended to keep on building dwellings, although at a rate lower than the 3,500 completed that year. In particular, prompted by the trend to smaller households, it aimed to cater for the increased demand for one-bedroomed dwellings. However, its most urgent priority was to halt the deterioration of the housing stock in the inner city. The back-to-backs of Birmingham may have been removed, but that did not mean that the problem of obsolescent housing had been solved. In 1979, over 100,000 of the city's houses were structures built before 1914. Most were tunnel-backs situated in the middle ring, and when they had been built they had provided good quality homes for better-paid working class Brummies. But by the late 1970s many of these structures were decaying, and their facilities were outdated and inadequate. 40,000 of them were listed as needing either substantial improvement or demolition, and a further 26,000 were likely to become sub-standard over the next five years if they were not improved. The council had rid itself of its inheritance of dreadful housing; now it had to address this difficulty if another slum problem was not to be its bequest to future Brummies.

Birmingham's urban renewal programme began in 1972 when the council designated 68 General Improvement Areas. They covered 62,000 houses which were to be retained and improved with virtually no demolition for the next 30 years. Additionally, it declared 28 Renewal Areas, later known as Housing Action Areas, embracing 15,000 dwellings. Here the council was to adopt a mixed approach of improvement and clearance. Since the turn of the century, when Nettleford had opened up courtyards in central Birmingham, reconditioning had been a vital aspect of the city's housing strategy. Sometimes it had been complemented by large-scale council-house building; at others it had been the sole or chief response to Birmingham's housing problem. This was so in the 1970s, when a harsher economic climate and changing ideas ensured that council-house building would decline drastically. In these circumstances, it proved beneficial that Birmingham had a long association with renovation and that it had pioneered improvement methods. Its tradition of innovation continued with the new technique of 'enveloping'. This was developed by the city's Environmental Health Department which was mostly responsible for urban renewal, and it meant that the outside - the envelope - of whole roads of older houses would be improved at no cost to their owners.

In the mid-1970s, Little Green was chosen as the testing ground for the then emerging concept of "urban renewal". Birmingham effectively pioneered this national policy which sought to reverse the decline wrought on our inner cities by decades of neglect and indifference .... More than 300 houses in the district have been renovated under an "envelope" scheme. (David Browne, Birmingham Evening Mail, 1984)

The enveloping of a road of nineteenth-century tunnel-back houses.
(Birmingham City Council Housing Department)

Not only was the political and financial climate unfavourable to massive redevelopment schemes, so too were the opinions of Brummies who lived in run-down properties. Many were owned by members of ethnic minorities who did not want to move away from the communities which had grown up since the 1950s. Enveloping, then, can be seen as an imaginative, sensitive and effective way of improving Birmingham's housing stock and its environment. However, its widespread adoption depended upon the success of the experimental schemes at Little Green, Small Heath and at Havelock, Saltley. Here the council re-slabbed pavements, re-surfaced roads, cleared waste land, pedestrianised streets and built play areas, as well as improved the outside of houses with new roofs, gutters and windows. Although the Labour government gave a generous 90% grant towards these external renovations, many householders could not afford to pay the 10% necessary for them to go ahead. Accordingly, Birmingham's Conservative-controlled council decided to pay this sum itself. The money proved well spent, and in 1979 the new Conservative government agreed with the council to jointly finance free outside improvements to 500 homes in Trafalgar (Moseley), Conway (Sparkbrook), and St Silas (Lozells). The facelifts cost £3,000 per house, and were expected to add 30 years to the life of the dwellings, whilst grants were available also for internal improvements.

A road of nineteenth-century tunnel-back houses after enveloping.
(Birmingham City Council Housing Department)

Enveloping has become a vital part of Birmingham's housing policy, but out-of-date dwellings are not restricted to inner-city areas. By the late 1970s, the 30,000 plus municipal houses built in the inter-war years were showing signs of old age, and in 1979 the council began a huge ten-year plan aimed at their modernisation. Following the recommendations of Richard Westlake, the city's Housing Officer, this was approached in a coherent and comprehensive fashion. Instead of tackling it piecemeal on a scattered system, it was carried out on a street-by-street basis, tied in to planned maintenance. Modernisation involved repairing the fabric of the house where necessary, for example putting on a new roof; rewiring; enlarging the kitchen to provide a kitchen cum breakfast room in non-parlour houses; and moving the bathroom upstairs. On average, it cost £5,000 per house and put 60 to 65 pence on rents, and whilst it was carried out tenants were moved temporarily - usually for eight weeks - in to "decant" houses. Part of the strategy of reconditioning included the conversion of some inter-war houses in to two self-contained, one-bedroomed flats. This allowed elderly tenants to stay in their area, and freed up houses elsewhere for families; and also it gave accommodation to single people who were now admitted to the housing register.

About 1,000 Birmingham council tenants will have their homes fully modernised this year in a 5 million facelift. It will be the first phase of a massive ten-year plan to spruce up the city's stock of more than 30,000 pre-war municipal houses. Most of them have outside toilets and what are described in a report as "antiquated facilities".

(Roy Smith, Birmingham Evening Mail, 1978)

Inter-war council house in Bierton Road, Garretts Green after it has been converted into two flats. (Birmingham City Council Housing Department)

Birmingham councillors have voted to tear down the rambling run-down warren of 266 problem flats in St Martin's, Highgate. And there was a prediction today that other unpopular, difficult-to-let blocks of flats will have to be demolished within the next five years. (Birmingham Evening Mail, 1979)

The clearance of St Martin's Flats, Emily Street, finished in 1939, demolished 1981.
(Birmingham Library Services)

Any hopes that councillors and Brummies have had that the city's housing problems have been solved seem to be dashed with a monotonous and unrelenting regularity. Each decade of the post-war years has been associated with a particular housing worry. The 1950s and 1960s are marked indelibly by the struggle to eliminate the city's back-to-backs; the 1970s and 1980s have been scarred by a need to grapple with the problems of a worsening housing stock in the inner city and on inter-war municipal estates; and unless central government grasps the nettle of bad housing, then the 1990s must be marred by the mounting difficulties posed by the legacy of high-rise flats and industrialised building. Indeed, the tocsin warning of the imminent approach of a new housing dilemma sounded in 1979, when it was decided to demolish the pre-war St Martin's flats in Emily Street, Highgate. Built with such high expectations just over 40 years previously, their short and unhappy life indicated the enormity of the predicament created by Birmingham's 429 blocks of post-war, multi-storey flats. There is an increasing knowledge of the structural defects of the industrialised building techniques used in them, and the time has come when they must be dealt with. Further, hundreds of inter-war houses built non-traditionally are crumbling and disintegrating, as chemicals and the climate affect substances like colliery waste which were used in their building.

Under both Conservative and Labour-led councils, Birmingham has striven to diminish the likelihood of the severe housing crisis which is threatened both by the mounting structural flaws of high-rise flats, and the social troubles associated with them. In 1979 it inaugurated a plan which aimed to encourage elderly people to move out of under-occupied council houses, so allowing swaps with families with children who lived in flats. The two blocks first converted were in Grove Road, Kings Heath, where 67 flats became warden-service homes. Each was fitted with an intercom alarm system linking the tenants with the warden, and an entry-phone network was installed to keep out vandals and intruders; whilst all the residents had use of a community room. The flats have proven popular with the elderly and now 35 blocks have been converted, whilst a 'concierge' scheme has been introduced to twelve other blocks. Another strategy adopted by the Housing Department with regard to multi-storey buildings has been to lop off the top two floors of four-storey maisonettes. This has created two-storey houses, as at Bennett Street and Johnstone Street, Lozells in 1983. However, not all high-rise flats can become warden-service towers, and most are too high to be suitable for lopping off. Furthermore, many of them are so unsound structurally that any form of conversion is most unlikely.

A pioneering plan to offer pensioners warden-service homes in converted multi-storey flats has been officially unveiled. City housing chiefs opened an experimental 40,000 conversion in two adjoining nine-storey blocks at Kings Heath in what is believed to be the first scheme of its kind in the country. (Birmingham Evening Mail, 1979)

'Top-lopping' of maisonettes in Johnson Street, Lozells.
(Birmingham City Council Housing Department)

The council once owned 156,000 properties. Now there are just 117,000 and it continues to sell at the rate of 1,300 a year. Nothing is being done to replace that stock. At the height of its building programme in the '60s the council was building 9,000 houses a year. Last year it constructed just 12.

(Keith Kendrick, Birmingham Evening Mail, 1990)

In 1985-1986 the council carried out an abseiling survey of its 427 tower blocks. This helped it ascertain the problems which affected them.
(Birmingham City Council Housing Department)

A recent abseiling survey revealed grave problems with many of Birmingham's tower blocks. One of the most serious is the loosening of cladding panels due to rusting metal ties and the effects of the atmosphere. This results in falling masonry, and many multi-storey flats have been surrounded by temporary fencing to prevent people from walking in the most hazardous places. In other blocks, tenants are plagued by serious dampness, or else they are endangered by defective concrete frames and bases. The cost of repairing those flats worst affected could be upwards of £500,000 each, but at the most it would add just 30 years to their life. Unsurprisingly, the council considers that demolition might be the most effective solution, both financially and socially; indeed, two blocks were knocked down at Northfield in 1986. However, whilst clearance might be desirable it is not necessarily advisable. Tower blocks house 25,000 tenants - 18% of the council's total; where would these people be rehoused if their homes were destroyed? The government's popular Right to Buy policy has brought home-ownership within reach of many working-class people, but at the same time council-owned dwellings have been reduced by 42,000 to 112,000. Consequently, fewer properties are available for transfer. Furthermore, cuts in government lending have meant that council resources have been directed at the pressing needs of repair, so that little or no money has been available for building.

Council-house sales have benefited many people and have contributed to a positive expansion in home ownership. Yet not everyone can afford to buy a house. If the council is to help housing associations meet the need for rented accommodation, it has to be able to build good-quality houses to replenish its stock. There is little sign of this happening, for in 1988/89 it completed just twelve homes. Of course, the city's housing situation is helped by enveloping and other improvement schemes. Redeveloped so optimistically just 40 years ago, Nechells is now part of Birmingham Heartlands, an Urban Development Agency which is making another attempt at regeneration. Here, too, the Bloomsbury Estate Management Board project is making improvements based on the wishes of tenants; and in Ladywood, government funding from the Estate Action initiative is helping to improve more dwellings. But Birmingham's long involvement with reconditioning shows that unless improvement schemes are accompanied by council-house building, then housing problems are deferred not solved. 70,000 private homes in the city are unfit, lack amenities or need renovation; and at least 226 high-rise flats need attention. Alone, improvement cannot defeat this urban blight. With on-going and thoughtfully planned council-house building, it may. This century, Birmingham has contended successfully with a dire housing problem inherited from its past. If council-house building is not begun in earnest, then dilapidated tower blocks and out-dated tunnel-backs may be our unwanted legacy to the future.

Brenda Dobson, of Birmingham City Council's resettlement team, said .... "Without new building there is only so much accommodation to go round."

(Keith Kendrick, Birmingham Evening Mail, 1990)

Highgate is the first of the new integrated concierge schemes. Here, the latest technology - developed with the advice of the Housing Department - has been used to improve the level of service to residents. (The Independent)

"The 1990s will be a decade of increasing consumerism in housing services which will mean the need to provide more and more choice for people not only in terms of the tenure of their home but in terms of the quality of services they receive.

For the City Council, this means not only maintaining its role as the major provider of council housing improving and enhancing its services in this regard but also seeking to provide other forms of housing to meet the varied needs of the citizens of Birmingham." (David Cowans, Deputy Director, Housing, Birmingham City Council Housing Department, 1990)

Tenants at Nechells who have voted 'yes' to involve themselves with the Bloomsbury Estate Management Board. This scheme is another 'first' for Birmingham and it gives tenants real control over the management of their estates.
(Birmingham City Council Housing Department)

Throughout its history, Birmingham Housing Department has had to deal with the dictates of reality, and has had to avoid futile involvement with wishful thinking. The challenges of the 1990s need to be confronted with the same sense of purpose. A renewal of council house building may be desirable, but financial restrictions make it unlikely. Consequently, the Housing Department must continue to be innovative in its response to housing problems and to the demand for community-based housing solutions. Few could argue against the movement for consumerism in rented housing with its aim of giving council tenants more control over their homes and their environment. Still, if it is to be successful then the city's housing chiefs have to indicate their willingness to listen to the voice of tenants and to abandon the concepts of social engineering previously so popular amongst planners. This they are doing. At the Stockfield Estate, Acocks Green, families have voted for the demolition of their 477 crumbling homes. In response, the Housing Department has sent in the bulldozers and has formed a partnership with Stockfield Residents, Bromford Housing Association and Halifax Building Society to build 425 new homes in a £24 million development. Derek Waddington, Director of Housing, is considering a similar community-based scheme for families living in decaying houses in Gospel Lane. No one can predict the future, but it seems certain that the Stockfield Road Estate will provide an example for a sensitive yet realistic housing policy for the 1990s.

FURTHER READING

Copies of most of the following books and unpublished manuscripts can be found in the Local Studies Department, Central Library, Birmingham. This is a treasure trove of information for anyone interested in Birmingham's history.

Working-class Life Stories

Walter Chinn, *From Victoria's Image* (unpublished manuscript)

Kathleen Dayus, *Her People* (London, 1982)
        Where There's Life (London, 1985)
        All My Days (London, 1988)

Jack Francis, *Pawnshops and Lard* (Leicester, 1989)

Syd Garrett, *I Remember . . . Tales of old Ladywood* (Birmingham, n.d)

Tom Golding, *96 years a Brummie* (Birmingham, 1986)
        The Brum We Knew (Birmingham, 1988)

Win Heywood, *My Mother's Story* (Northwood, 1986)

Taffy Lewis, *"Any Road". Pictures of Small Heath, Sparkbrook and further afield 1902-39*
        (Birmingham 1979)

Alan Mahar (ed.), *Memories of Balsall Heath, Highgate and Sparkbrook* (Birmingham, 1983)
        Writing It Down Befores It's All Gone; working class life in Balsall Heath between the wars (Birmingham 1984)

Leslie Mayell, *The Birmingham I Remember* (Padstow, 1980)
        Further Memories of Birmingham (Padstow, 1982)

Lily Need, *Struggling Manor* (unpublished manuscript)

Ruth M. Slade, *Annie, Margaret, Ruth, Doreen, Nicola; A Family History*
        (unpublished manuscript, 1989)

Will Thorne, *My Life's Battles* (First published 1925, new edition, London, 1989)

Howard Williamson, *Toolmaking and Politics. The Life of Ted Smallbone - an oral history* (Birmingham, 1987)

Books on Working-class Life in Birmingham

Carl Chinn, *They Worked All Their Lives: Women of the Urban Poor in England, 1880-1939* (Manchester, 1988)

Ronald K. Moore, *Up The Terrace Down Aston and Lozells* (Birmingham, 1988)

Victor Price, *Aston Remembered, Yesterday and Today* (Studley, 1989)
The People's Century, Birmingham 1889-1989 (Birmingham, 1989)
The Summer Lane And Newtown Of The Years Between The Wars 1918-1939 (Birmingham, 1985)

Novels on Working-class Life in Birmingham

Walter Allen, *All In A Lifetime* (First published 1959, new edition, London, 1986)

John Douglas, *A Walk Down Summer Lane* (London, 1983)

Histories of Birmingham

Conrad Gill, *History of Birmingham Volume I. Manor and Borough to 1865* (London, 1952)
Asa Briggs, *History of Birmingham Volume II. Borough and City 1865-1938* (London, 1952)
Anthony Sutcliffe & Roger Smith, *History of Birmingham Volume III. Birmingham 1939-1970* (London, 1974)

Victor Skipp, *The Making of Victorian Birmingham* (Birmingham, 1983)

John Thackray Bunce, *History of the Corporation of Birmingham, Volume I* (Birmingham, 1878)
John Thackray Bunce, *History of the Corporation of Birmingham, Volume II* (Birmingham, 1885)
Charles Anthony Vince, *History of the Corporation of Birmingham, Volumes III and IV* (Birmingham, 1902)
Joseph Trevor Jones, *History of the Corporation of Birmingham, Volume V* (Birmingham, 1940)

Housing in Birmingham

Birmingham Planning Department, *Developing Birmingham 1889-1989. 100 years of City Planning*, (Birmingham, 1989)

Bournville Village Trust, *Bournville Village Trust 1900-1955* (Birmingham, 1955) *When We Build Again. A Study Based on Research Into Conditions of Living and Working in Birmingham* (London, 1941)

F. Margaret Fenter, *Copec Adventure. The Story of the Birmingham Copec House Improvement Society* (Birmingham, 1960)

Housing in General

John Burnett, *A Social History of Housing 1815-1985* (2nd edition, London, 1986)

Some books and articles which are mentioned in this book are not included in this list of further reading. Most can be found in Birmingham Central Library, whilst the annual reports of the city's Medical Officer of Health are in the Local Studies Department.

Birmingham in Photographs

The Local Studies Department, Birmingham Central Library, contains the Slum Collection, an evocative collection of photographs of back-to-back houses and courtyards taken in 1904.

Michael Glasson, *City Children, Birmingham Children at Work and Play 1900-1930* (Birmingham, 1985)

Dorothy McCulla (itn.), *Victorian and Edwardian Birmingham from old photographs* (London, 1973)

John Whybrow and Rachel Waterhouse, *How Birmingham became a Great City* (Birmingham, 1976)